TEACH YOUR KIDS ABOUT MUSIC

TEACH YOUR KIDS ABOUT MUSIC

An Activity Handbook
for Parents and
Teachers
Using Children's
Literature

RUBY CHRONINGER

WALKER AND COMPANY
NEW YORK

First published in the United States of America in 1994 by Walker Publishing Company, Inc.

Published simultaneously in Canada by Thomas Allen & Son Canada, Limited, Markham, Ontario

Library of Congress Cataloging-in-Publication Data
Chroninger, Ruby.
    Teach your kids about music : an activity handbook for parents and teachers using children's literature / Ruby Chroninger.
        p. cm.
    Discography:
    Includes bibliographical references and indexes.
    ISBN 0-8027-1280-0   —ISBN 0-8027-7410-5 (pbk.)
    1. Music—Instruction and study—Juvenile.   2. School music—Instruction and study—Activity programs.   3. Music and literature.
    4. Children's literature.   I. Title.
    MT1.C539   1993
    372.87'044—dc20   93-8081
                                                          CIP
                                                          MN

DESIGN BY GLEN M. EDELSTEIN

Printed in the United States of America

10   9   8   7   6   5   4   3   2   1

For My Children,
Lauren and David,
and with Deepest Love to My Husband,
Stephen

Contents

Preface

THIS BOOK IS WRITTEN FOR PARENTS AND TEACHERS OF YOUNG children (in preschool through the third grade). It combines the teaching of music with children's literature through fun, creative activities. Its premise is simple: kids learn the language of music by using the language, poetry, and rhyme of excellent children's books. A brief description of how this book came into being is in order.

During the last ten years, while teaching music both privately and in the classroom, I have frequently observed classroom teachers including songs and recordings in their lesson plans. While this practice serves many useful academic purposes and is highly recommended, it is also important to introduce young children to musical concepts and to give them the opportunity to participate in a variety of musical experiences. But the classroom teacher rarely makes a point of discussing the rhythm or the melody of a song or the significance of music within our culture. Concepts of this sort are usually left to the music teacher. Unfortunately, many preschools and early elementary classrooms lack the assistance or guidance of a music specialist. Thus, many young children are never exposed to a complete, well-rounded musical curriculum.

After I discussed my observations and concerns with numerous classroom teachers, it became apparent to me that many teachers do not always feel comfortable covering musical concepts. They cited a lack of training in this area, a lack of resources, and, most important, a lack of time.

To help alleviate these problems, I decided to create a book that could be used by the adult with little or no musical background; a book that would also promote the use of materials (such as children's books) that perhaps were already being used in the classroom, saving the teacher preparation time and classroom time. I believed the integration of music and children's literature would be a successful endeavor because numerous similarities exist between the two subjects.

As I worked on this project, I tried out the activities on my daughter, who was four at the time. Then they were sampled by a group of classroom teachers whose students were in kindergarten through third grade. I later used the activities with my son, who is age five, as well as with the three- to five-year-old children in my preschool music classes. It was a joy to see how easily the children grasped the musical concepts and exciting to know that they were doing so while listening to some of the best stories written for young people.

My editor, Mary Kennan Herbert, suggested that I rewrite the manuscript so that parents, as well as teachers, could use it. Having taught my own children music by using many of the activities, I agreed that this was an excellent idea.

This book is designed to assist parents, teachers, and all who work with young children in helping them discover the joys of music through use of their favorite stories and children's books. The activities featured in this book introduce the young child to the basics of music and involve the child in the development of musical skills such as singing, movement, instrumention, listening, and composing. *Teach Your Kids About Music* can also help expand children's awareness of America's multicultural music and assist each child in the development of musical appreciation. No musical background is required. Even if you cannot read music, this book is designed to give you a practical and creative approach to teaching it. The activities are organized so that they can be used with an individual child or with a whole classroom of budding young musicians.

The book includes numerous activities, an annotated bibliography of exceptional general literature for children, an annotated bibliography of outstanding musical literature for children, and an annotated discography. In addition, it has a subject guide, which will be most useful for teachers who may wish to plan units of study around the activities, a glossary of musical terms used in the activities, and an index. Numerous cross references make the book easy to use. Also included are tips and ideas for finding additional resources, locating private music teachers, assisting your child at home with lessons, supporting your school music program, and much more.

Most of all, this book offers innovative ways for parents and children to have fun together. Kindergarten teachers, parents of toddlers, classroom aides, and volunteers—everyone can enjoy and create music. Kids too. Here are fifty-nine ways to get started in your musical adventures.

Acknowledgments

IT IS WITH SINCERE APPRECIATION THAT I THANK PROFESSORS Arthur Hills, Charles Rhinehart, and Larry Snyder at Sonoma State University in Rohnert Park, California, who encouraged me to pursue the idea of publishing this work.

A special thank-you is extended to the participating kindergarten through third grade teachers and to their students who sampled the activities during the early stages of my work.

To the librarians of the Ruben Salazar Library at Sonoma State University, the Rohnert Park Public Library, and the Sonoma County Central Library—thank you for your assistance.

To Ruth Gordon and Millie Lee, I am grateful for your suggestions and support.

I wish to extend my appreciation to the following individuals for reading a draft of the manuscript and giving me additional ideas: Arthur Dougherty, retired arts coordinator of the San Ramon Valley Unified School District, Danville, California; Jane Dougherty, library assistant of the Montevideo Elementary School in San Ramon, California; and Melissa Hensley, primary teacher of the Rainbow Bridge Montessori School in Cotati, California.

To my current editor, Mary Kennan Herbert, thank you for the guidance you supplied to this first-time writer.

My deepest appreciation is extended to my brother and sister-in-law, Bill Osburn and Cindy Meyer, for helping with computer technicalities.

To my husband, Stephen, thank you for your understanding, love, encouragement, and computer assistance. To my children, Lauren and David, I will always treasure the countless hours we spend listening to stories, singing songs, and sharing in the creation of ideas.

PART 1

CHAPTER ONE

Why Use Children's Books to Teach Music?

I F YOU ARE INTERESTED IN BRINGING MUSIC INTO THE LIVES OF young children, be they your own or those in your class, and if you also enjoy the experience of reading to, or with, your youngsters, this book is written for you!

You may have, at one time or another, thought about involving your children in activities such as singing, movement, playing instruments, composing, and the like. But perhaps you weren't quite sure how to go about doing so. If you are a teacher, you may have given up on many ideas because of a lack of resources, or perhaps because you have felt, as many do, that there is no time to prepare for yet another subject. Even those teachers who include music in their lesson plans often do so only to supplement a nonmusical unit of study. Let me explain this in more detail, for it will be of interest to both teachers and parents.

If you are a teacher, imagine that you are teaching a unit that focuses on the seasons and the changes that occur in nature. If you are a parent, you might be teaching your own kids the same thing. You may teach children a song having to do with fall or spring. The objective here is not to increase the understanding of a musical concept but to use the words of the song to enhance observations of nature. Over the years, I have noticed that this practice of rote singing has taken the place of a complete musical curriculum in the preschool and lower grades. There are even a scattering of music teachers who have fallen into this habit.

Although rote singing as a supplement to other subjects should not be abandoned, it is also necessary to introduce musical concepts such as rhythm, pitch, and harmony. It is important to discuss songs in terms of their purpose in our culture.

How do you go about doing this if you have little experience in music? How do you purchase music resources if the funds are simply not there? How do you fit one more topic into the busy school day? It is easy to see why many classroom teachers have simply thrown up their hands in frustration and given in to the practice of inserting a song here or there to "make things fun for the kids." At the greatest disadvantage are those classroom teachers who have no music specialist with whom to consult when music questions or concerns arise.

Because many preschools and elementary schools do not provide a music education (that is, they do not teach musical *concepts*), parents interested in enriching their children's musical studies are now seeking alternatives. Many parents enroll their children in music classes independent from the school, while others give their children private lessons.

Now that I myself am in the position of teaching private lessons and preschool music classes, I have found that parents also have a great many questions. Some wonder if their children are *ready* for a musical experience. Others wish to know what they can do at home *before* starting their child in music. Some ask what they can do to supplement their child's music instruction once it has begun. Many parents have even told me that because they have no musical training, they fear that their involvement will have a negative impact on their youngster's musical studies.

Must the classroom teacher or parent be able to read music? Must you have a wonderful voice and/or play an instrument to provide exciting and solid musical experiences for children? *Absolutely not!* Although I certainly recommend that you become musically literate for your own personal growth, your limited background should not stop you from becoming a musical partner with your child. In recent years, a number of published articles have even provided the nonmusical teacher as well as the parent with ideas for introducing simple, yet instructive, musical activities.

Over the years, it has become apparent to me that what parents and classroom teachers need is a book that focuses on the teaching of musical concepts and the development of musical skills which does not require a background in music, and which—most of all—can provide fun for adult and child alike. I thought that adults might be more successful and the experience more enjoyable if the musical activities could be part of a daily occurrence such as reading aloud to one's children.

Why use children's books to teach music? To answer this question, let's go back for a moment to our example of teaching a classroom unit on changing seasons. As a teacher, or as a parent, you may have discussed how the leaves change color in the fall and how the trees bare their leaves. You have undoubtedly supplemented this explanation with a picture book focusing on the same subject. You are now ready to sing or listen to a song as a further exploration of the topic. Stop for a moment and consider the song you are about to teach.

Why not select one that has a falling melody—a tune that starts high and ends low—and have the children fall slowly to the ground (like falling leaves) as they sing? Why not take a few moments and discuss the shape of this melody, as well as the shape of the children's corresponding movements? You have just introduced an important musical concept, that of melodic contour. You did not need to be able to read music to do so; you did not need expensive resources; and you spent very little extra time preparing for the lesson. You have integrated two art forms, music and literature, in an interesting, creative, and fun-filled manner. Literature on the subject suggests that a program encompassing music, movement, and other subjects—language arts, as an example—can and should be implemented by the classroom teacher.

As a parent, you are provided with numerous opportunities during the course of the day to spontaneously involve your children in musical activities. When my children and I attend concerts or movies, my youngest usually ends up on my lap. While we listen to the musical selections being performed, I often tap the rhythm on his knees, hands, or shoulders. In return, he often rests his hands on mine so that he too is a participant in my responses. When I stop, he often continues to tap the rhythm on his own. Later, I may read him a book that has a lilting rhythmic flavor, or I may read him a story about musicians or performers. I have taken little time out of my day to engage my child in a musical activity, and I have integrated literature and music. Since children innately respond to music, parents may easily find opportunities to involve children in such activities.

As I wrote this book, I found that the idea of combining music and children's literature to achieve musical objectives is a valid one for many reasons. Let us take a look at a few of the many positive results.

Music and literature, as well as art forms in general, have certain characteristics that are alike. And when any two art forms are studied together, the similar concepts shared by the two are reinforced. The child strengthens his or her understandings and skills in *both* subject areas. What are the common characteristics between music and literature?

As was the case with my own son, children eagerly respond to rhythm. As children move, play, and speak, they do so in a rhythmic fashion. Rhythm, of course, can be found in children's literature as well as in music. Teachers and parents will find that the reinforcement of rhythm when literature and music are combined captures the child's interest. The child attaches a deeper meaning to the stories and the songs.

When music and literature are combined, a number of patterns spring to life. Examples include melodic patterns, rhythmic patterns, grammatical patterns, and speech patterns. When children work with these patterns in combination, the outcome is a better understanding of all areas involved. Two other characteristics common among the arts are repetition and form.

Like music, children's literature is filled with phrases and favorite words that are frequently repeated. Since children possess a seemingly natural love for repetition, this element may be used as a vehicle for furthering an understanding of both music and literature. Song lyrics can be used to introduce children to poetry. In doing so, you may discuss rhythm and repetition in addition to the element of form—the way in which a musical selection or literary example is put together.

Besides rhythm, patterning, repetition, and form, there are

additional musical elements which may be added when reading aloud to one's child. Those characteristics that make a
storytelling experience expressive are in themselves musical
elements. As you read a story to your child, you may alter your
voice in a number of ways. You may slow down or speed up. You
may read some passages loud and others soft. As the content
of the story is made clearer because of this expression, the
child is exposed to musical elements that will be more easily
identifiable when listening to music or performing music at a
later date. Applying musical elements to the choral reading of
poetry may strengthen the development of children's higher-
order thinking skills.

Earlier, I mentioned how classroom teachers may use music
to introduce and reinforce other topics being covered in the
classroom. Music and literature may both be thought of as a
means for communicating ideas. This is yet another reason to
integrate the two, providing, of course, that one realizes the
value of music as a subject in itself.

Music may be thought of as a form of literature. One can
study and classify musical selections in regard to types and
place in history, just as one does with literature. The arts in
general may be studied in terms of common themes and historical periods, as well as in terms of a common geographical
location. Many works of art are by their very nature a mixture
of art forms such as the musical, for example. It is no wonder
that authors of children's literature have recognized the pow-
erful results of *combining* art forms in children's books.

Singing and reading can go hand in hand. A new and exciting type of children's literature has emerged in recent years.
Many folk songs, ballads, patriotic songs, holiday songs, and
the like have been converted into children's picture books.
Many believe that this form of literature is an outstanding addition to the classroom. Parents, of course, may find these
books to be particularly useful as well, for they encourage
young children to sing along with the stories. Such literature
provides children with illustrative examples of relating art
forms, stimulating their interest in both books and songs.

Teachers of older children and teenagers may successfully
use in their music classes novels that focus on others their age

who are involved in musical activities. Such a study introduces youngsters to the feelings and actions of the musician, and possibly to the musical jargon used among music makers.

Obviously, one can see that the combination of music and literature may strengthen a child's understanding of musical elements and at the same time expose a child to wonderful books that are based on specific musical genres or that focus on musicians. It should also be noted that a number of authors (see References) have mentioned the positive effects of music on various components of the language arts curriculum. When we look collectively at what they've said, we see that music enhances reading, creative expression and writing, vocabulary, listening skills, speaking, spelling, handwriting . . . and more!

While working as a classroom music teacher in a small public school, I had the personal experience of realizing how significant the effect of music is on the entire language arts curriculum. After introducing the concept of "syllabification" to her class, the combination first/second grade teacher found that her children were already quite adept at breaking words into syllables. When she asked the class how they had learned this skill, their explanation was that they had practiced it in music class! In a way, they had. In music class, we had just finished writing original compositions. The children had discovered that they needed to break each word into separate sounds (syllables) in order for the words to match up with the rhythms they had created. It was exciting for me to know that the children were able to make the connection between their musical studies and their "regular" work in the classroom. As you use the activities in this book, your children may make similar discoveries.

The goal here, however, is to provide numerous activities that will allow you to combine music and children's literature to specifically teach *musical* concepts and to strengthen *musical* skills.

In each chapter, main goals are suggested. Activities then follow that are designed to aid in the teaching of these main goals. The activities are presented in the following format:

General literature for children. Includes a listing of books that can be used in the activity. A description of these books is given in the Annotated Bibliography of General Literature for children. Since some of the activities are meant to serve as the basis for later experiences, or as follow-up reinforcements, not all activities will require the use of related literature.

Materials. If the activity requires materials such as paper, crayons, and magazines, they are listed here.

Directions. Detailed directions are then provided in easy-to-understand language.

Variations. Wherever possible, variations of the activity are presented to give you more options.

Suggested musical resources. Books with a musical theme, as well as recordings that are integrated in the activities, are listed under this heading. These resources are thoroughly explained in the Annotated Bibliography of Musical Literature for Children and the Annotated Discography.

The Appendix presents a subject guide that will be helpful in overall planning.

It is to be understood that although this book provides a well-rounded approach to teaching basic musical concepts and strengthening musical skills, it is not a substitute for a detailed musical curriculum taught by a qualified music instructor. I firmly believe that music is not a frill in the classroom and that it should be a required part of the curriculum for all children.

Music does not, however, need to be left only to the specialist. We may all be participants, and we may all make music part of learning. This book is a guide for doing so.

CHAPTER TWO

Activities Involving Sound Awareness and the Concepts of Duration and Pitch

THIS CHAPTER INTRODUCES CHILDREN TO A VARIETY OF sounds. The musical concepts of duration and pitch are also explored as children learn that sounds have specific characteristics. Here are a few points to keep in mind when presenting the activities.

- ● *Sound Awareness*
  Not only can sounds be created, they can also be altered.

- ● *Duration*
  The steady, ongoing pulse in music is known as the *beat*. Beats may be strong or weak, and the way in which they are grouped is referred to as *meter*. There are long sounds and short sounds, as well as long and short silences which may be combined in a variety of ways to create the *rhythm*.

- ● *Pitch*
  There are high sounds and low sounds, and these tones may be combined to create a tune, or melody.

SOUND AWARENESS

PRIOR TO DISCUSSING SPECIFIC CHARACTERISTICS OF SOUNDS (high/low, long/short), children will benefit from a general introduction to the numerous sounds in our environment. They begin by focusing attention on sounds that are often found in children's literature. This lays the foundation for an exploration of the sounds heard in and around the classroom or home.

Children enjoy experimenting with ways of creating sounds through the use of their bodies and handmade instruments. They can also experience the fun of capturing various sounds on tape and having others guess the sources. By participating in these activities, children will learn that sounds can be created in a variety of ways and that they can also be modified.

1. USING CHILDREN'S BOOKS TO INTRODUCE THE STUDY OF SOUNDS

General literature for children:
One or more of the following books: *Charlie and the Chocolate Factory*; *Charlotte's Web*; *Danny, the Champion of the World*; *If You Lived at the Time of the Great San Francisco Earthquake*; *If You Sailed on the Mayflower*; *Sing a Song of Popcorn: Every Child's Book of Poems*; *The Sky Is Full of Song*; *Too Much Noise*; *Who's in Rabbit's House? A Masai Tale*; *Why Mosquitoes Buzz in People's Ears: A West African Tale*, or any other favorite stories that deal with a variety of environmental sounds.

Directions:
After reading one of the above books (or a chapter from one of the longer books), ask children to name various sounds that are noted in the story.

Next, have children listen to the various sounds in their own environment at home or at school. Ask: "What sounds do you hear in the house?" or "What sounds do you hear in the classroom?" Make a list of their responses.

Variation:

If using this activity with a group of older children, parents or teachers may wish to make a game of who can name the most sounds heard. Provide each child with a piece of paper and instruct kids to list as many sounds as possible in a specified amount of time.

To make this game more interesting, you may want to list sounds that one would hear in such places as a forest, a zoo, or a fire station.

2. MAKING A SOUND COLLAGE

Materials:

Old magazines, scissors, and paste.

Directions:

Supply children with a variety of old magazines, and have them select a number of pictures of items that produce sounds (cars, animals, people, machines, etc.). Cut out these pictures and paste them onto a large piece of paper, overlapping the cutouts to form a collage. A sound collage of the items or creatures mentioned in a story from Activity 1 would be particularly suitable at this time.

Discuss the various sounds that are shown. For added fun, see who can do the best imitations of the items pictured. Display these pictures at home or in the classroom.

3. PRODUCING SOUNDS WITH BODY PARTS

Directions:

Ask children to demonstrate what kinds of sounds can be created with hands. Their responses may include clapping hands, snapping fingers, and slapping hands against knees.

Next, have children demonstrate sounds that can be made with feet (stomps, taps, etc.). Experiment with sounds that can be produced with the tongue, lips, or cheeks.

Have children pretend they are characters from the story read in Activity 1. Ask them to make the sounds that the character might produce.

Finally, put on any favorite recording, and encourage children to accompany it with claps, snaps, or other such sounds. After a few sessions, you may notice that children enjoy combining sounds such as stomps with claps or tongue clicks with snaps. This creativity should be encouraged.

4. CREATING HANDMADE DRUMS

General literature for children:
From Abenaki to Zuni: A Dictionary of Native American Tribes; *Small Wolf*; or any other book on Native Americans.

Materials:
Oatmeal boxes, salt boxes, or coffee cans; crayons; tape and construction paper.

Directions:
Children can create handmade drums by covering the oatmeal boxes, salt boxes, or coffee cans with construction paper. The young child may need some assistance with this process. Children may then wish to decorate the outside of their drums with drawings, feathers, or other materials.

Have children experiment with ways of changing the sounds created by these instruments. If they hold the drum close to their body and strike it, does it sound the same? If they cut a hole in the bottom, does this change the sound? You don't need to be an expert on sound production to assist children with these simple experiments.

Next, simply allow children to enjoy the sounds they can create. Put on a recording, and encourage them to play along with the music. Don't worry if what you hear isn't exactly musical. Remember, this is an introductory lesson to show that instrumental sounds can be created and altered. Have fun and experiment yourself!

This activity serves as a perfect example of how musical activities may be combined with the study of another subject—with the help of children's literature. If studying Native Americans, for example, you may want to read the book *Small Wolf* to children or gather information on various tribes using the book *From Abenaki to Zuni: A Dictionary of Native American Tribes*. Next, turn the oatmeal boxes into Indian drums using illustrations of Indian symbols as a guide (refer to *American Indian Music and Musical Instruments*).

Variation:

Rhythm instruments, those that are struck or shaken, can be made out of all kinds of ordinary household items. Ask children to select a variety of articles from around the house with which to create musical instruments. Such instruments may be extremely basic. For example, beans placed inside a container will rattle when shaken. (The books listed below provide additional information on making handmade instruments.) Remember to keep these instruments handy for later activities. They will be especially useful when we discuss the concept of tone color.

Suggested musical resources:

Books: *American Indian Music and Musical Instruments*; *Making Musical Things: Improvised Instruments*.

5. MAKING A TAPE OF SOUND EFFECTS

Materials:

Any recording that features a variety of sound effects (see recording listed below), a tape recorder, and a blank cassette.

Directions:

In preparation for this activity, first play a recording containing numerous sound effects. Children can have fun guessing the sound source for each example.

Next, have children create their own recordings (tapes) of sounds heard either at home or at school. Children who work on this project at home may wish to have other family members guess the sounds on their recording. If this is done as a class project, invite a guest in to guess the sounds represented on the tape.

This is the type of activity that children will enjoy working on for hours. There are an endless number of items that they will find fun and interesting to record, such as other children playing at recess, birds chirping, or the quiet purring of a pet cat.

Variation:

Create a tape that contains only the sounds mentioned in the literature from Activity 1. Then play the tape in the background when listening to the story at a later date or when presenting a dramatization of the story.

Suggested musical resource:

Recording: *Sound Effects* (there are a number of recordings in this series).

THE COMPONENTS OF DURATION: BEAT, METER, AND RHYTHM

AS CHILDREN TOOK PART IN ACTIVITIES 3 AND 4, YOU MAY HAVE noticed that their responses to music varied from time to time. Occasionally, when they clapped, moved, or played instruments, they may have done so in a consistent, steady fashion. If so, they were undoubtedly responding to the underlying pulse in music which we refer to as the beat.

If it appeared that they stressed certain beats and not others, they may have been responding to the meter. Meter is the natural grouping of strong (accented) and weak (unaccented) beats into sets. More often, however, they may have reacted to the combinations produced by sounds and silences of various lengths, or what is known as the rhythm.

It should be obvious that because these components are so interwoven, it is perfectly natural for children to sometimes respond to one component and at other times respond to another.

In the activities that follow, therefore, each will be treated as a separate entity to encourage a solid understanding of the components of duration—of how music moves through time.

BEAT

To help children understand the concept of a steady beat, have them search through stories for illustrations of objects that move in a steady fashion or produce a steady sound such as a kangaroo hopping or a clock ticking. Then list items in the children's own environment that do the same. Next, introduce children to visual representations of the beat, and allow them the opportunity to respond to these. Activities 6 and 7 show how this material may be presented.

6. *USING CHILDREN'S BOOKS TO INTRODUCE THE STUDY OF BEAT*

Materials:

Any favorite book from the general literature list that contains illustrations of items that keep a steady beat or produce a steady sound (a faucet dripping, a child jumping, etc.).

Directions:

After you have read a favorite story, point out to children the fact that some of the illustrations feature items that move in a constant, steady motion or that produce a steady sound. For example, there may be pictures of children swinging or riding on a seasaw. These are steady motions. Go through the book a second time, and reexamine the illustrations in more detail.

After you have identified additional items in the story, see if a child can now name objects in his or her own environment that keep a steady beat. Examples that have been noted by my own students include windshield wipers, a turn signal on a car, and the flashing lights on a VCR.

These creative answers all came from four- and five-year-old children!

7. FOLLOWING THE GREEN LIGHTS

Materials:
Eight green circles made from paper or felt.

Directions:
Tell children that the green circles are to be thought of as the green lights found on a traffic light. Every time you point to a circle, they will "get to go" by clapping their hands.

Lay the green lights out in the pattern illustrated below. In a steady fashion, point to each circle and say the word *clap* or *go* each time you point to a circle.

```
O    O
Clap Clap
O    O
Clap Clap
O    O
Clap Clap
O    O
Clap Clap
```

After some practice, you will find that kids have little difficulty following along. Once children are able to clap in a steady fashion, they are ready to learn the term *beat*. Say the word *beat* each time you point to a circle.

This exercise is useful not only because it involves children in the process of keeping a steady pulse, but also because it introduces them to the idea that music moves in groups of beats. Moreover, it is also excellent preparation for the process of learning to read from left to right and top to bottom.

On another day, review the literature selected for Activity 6 and create felt cutouts of the items identified as those that keep a steady beat. If, for example, children found an illustration of a ticking clock in one of the stories, create a felt cutout that looks like this clock. Use the cutouts in place of the green circles when reviewing this activity.

Variations:

Experiment with different ways of responding to each beat. For example, kids may wish to clap for the first circle and snap for the second, or stomp for the first circle and nod for the second.

Another variation is to have the children keep the beat on the rhythm instruments they constructed in Activity 4.

METER

Once children have participated in the above activities and can successfully respond to the beat, it is a perfect time to introduce the concept of meter—the idea that there are natural groupings of strong and weak beats. At this stage, children may simply be told that music moves in sets of beats and that the first beat of each set is heavy.

A waltz, for example, moves in groups of three (**1** 2 3, **1** 2 3), with the first count being stronger than the second and third. Present this example to the children. Make sure you accent the first count when doing so.

This introduction lays the foundation for Activity 8.

8. COUNTING IN TWO, THREE, AND FOUR

Materials:

Thirty-six felt circles or thirty-six felt cutouts of items found in a children's story (these should be items that produce a steady sound or move to a steady beat).

Directions:

Lay out the objects in the patterns illustrated below. Children can count and clap the circles in each example. At the same time, ask the children to demonstrate the accented, first count of each line by creating a large movement (bending their knees, stretching hands high, or jumping). This movement will call attention to the beginning of each group and to the fact that there are strong beats (accented) and weak beats (unaccented) in music.

Example A	*Example B*	*Example C*
O O	O O O	O O O O
1 2	1 2 3	1 2 3 4
O O	O O O	O O O O
1 2	1 2 3	1 2 3 4
O O	O O O	O O O O
1 2	1 2 3	1 2 3 4
O O	O O O	O O O O
1 2	1 2 3	1 2 3 4

After they can count and clap these examples successfully and can respond appropriately to the accented and unaccented beats, see if they can play the examples on the instruments that were created in Activity 4. Make sure they continue to accent count 1 of each line.

RHYTHM

If this is a child's first exposure to music, you will find that it is not necessary to discuss quarter notes, eighth rests, flags, and the like in order for the child to learn a great deal about the lengths of various notes and rests. Prior to any technical discussion of this sort, the child may simply be told that there are long tones, short tones, and long and short silences in music.

The adult does not need to know how to read music in order to guide the child through this learning experience. These ideas can be presented in entertaining, creative ways by focusing on the rhythms found in songs, poetry, and fingerplays.

9. ECHO CLAPPING FAVORITE SONGS

Directions:
Begin by first clapping combinations of long sounds, short sounds, and rests. As you clap, say *short* when you clap a short note, say *long* and clasp your hands together to illus-

trate a long sound, and whisper the word *rest* while swaying hands apart when you arrive at a silence. Ask children to echo this clapping pattern. Now change places: the kids create a clapped line, and you repeat it.

Next, sing a favorite song together. Then sing and clap the song by yourself. Clap every syllable of every word, and sway your hands to illustrate the silences (rests). In this way, children are learning to feel the silence even though it is not heard. Have a child sing the song and clap the rhythm with you.

For additional practice, clap each line of the song separately without singing. Have children echo you. You might try mixing the lines up to see if a child can guess which line of the song is being clapped. Finally, clap the rhythm of another known song, and see if children can guess the name of it. If there are specific combinations that repeat themselves, point this out. This activity lays the groundwork for Activity 10.

Variation:

At this point, it would be excellent practice to reinforce the difference between beat and rhythm. Ask children to sing and clap the rhythm of a favorite song. Then have them sing the song again while clapping the beat. Try this exercise with a variety of selections to illustrate the difference between the two concepts.

10. INTEGRATING CHILDREN'S POETRY WITH THE STUDY OF RHYTHM

General literature for children:

Black Is Brown Is Tan; *Brown Bear, Brown Bear, What Do You See?*; *Chickens Aren't the Only Ones*; *Goodnight Moon*; *A House Is a House for Me*; *It's Halloween*; *The New Kid on the Block*; *The Random House Book of Mother Goose: A Treasury of 306 Timeless Nursery Rhymes*; *Sing a Song of Popcorn: Every Child's Book of Poems*; or any other favorite book that features poetry or rhyme.

Directions:

Once children are aware of long sounds, short sounds, and rests, discovering the existence of these items in poetry will reinforce their understanding of rhythm. Select a book or poem from the list above, and read it aloud. As you speak, stress the lengths of the notes and/or the rests.

Next, recite the first line of one of the poems, and ask children to repeat the line. Make sure they repeat the poem expressively by stressing the rhythm. Then clap the rhythm of the same line, and have children echo clap. Clap the rhythm of another line, and see if a child can guess which line was performed.

11. EXPLORING RHYTHMS IN FINGERPLAYS

Materials:

A collection of songs or poems with hand movements (see below for collections of fingerplays).

Directions:

Select a fingerplay and teach it to children. You may want to select a fingerplay that deals with a subject covered in one of the poems from Activity 10. If you read a poem about a spider, for example, you can teach the fingerplay called "The Itsy, Bitsy Spider." When performing the fingerplay, emphasize the rhythm by speaking expressively and by moving fingers directly to the syllables. It is very easy to slip into the habit of only moving to the beat. Instead move your fingers as you speak *every* syllable of *every* word. Rest your fingers when you are not speaking, to illustrate the rests. Point out to children that patterns of movement may be created to correspond with the repetitive rhythmic patterns that may be present.

Variation:

Have children create their own fingerplays based on the poems or rhymes from Activity 10. Make sure that they stress the lengths of the sounds and silences.

Suggested musical resources:

Song collections: *American Folk Songs for Children in Home, School, and Nursery School: A Book for Children, Parents, and Teachers*; *Do Your Ears Hang Low? Fifty More Musical Fingerplays*; *Eye Winker, Tom Tinker, Chin Chopper: Fifty Musical Fingerplays*; *Singing Bee: A Collection of Favorite Children's Songs*.

12. LISTENING TO PARTICIPATION RECORDINGS THAT STRESS RHYTHM

Materials:

Any recordings that contain listener participation activities involving rhythm (see below).

Directions:

Play a recording emphasizing the lengths of various sounds and silences through participation activities. Have children take part in any recorded exercises that focus on echoing rhythms with their voices or with instruments, or that focus on demonstrating rhythms using movement (crawling for long sounds, hopping for short sounds, standing still for rests).

Suggested musical resources:

Recordings: *Play Your Instruments and Make a Pretty Sound*; *Rhythms of Childhood*; *You'll Sing a Song and I'll Sing a Song*.

THE CONCEPT OF PITCH

BECAUSE TODAY'S CHILDREN ARE BEING RAISED IN A VAST TECH-nological society, many of them may find the concept of pitch a very confusing one at first. We all know that when a child turns "up" the television or turns "down" the radio, a change of dynamics (a change of volume) is occurring. In the child's mind, *up* or *high* is associated with louder, and *down* or *low* with softer.

In music, however, the terms *high* and *low* refer to pitch and not to dynamics. It is important, therefore, to be on the alert for any possible confusion when involving children in activities focusing on the concept of pitch.

In learning about pitch, children will make good use of children's books and be encouraged to listen for high sounds and low sounds in their environments. They will find high and low sounds on keyboard instruments and move their bodies to illustrate a melody. Finally, they will create their own stories and then read them, using high and low voices to represent the characters in their stories.

13. INTEGRATING PITCH WITH CHILDREN'S BOOKS

General literature for children:
Black Is Brown Is Tan; *Charlie and the Chocolate Factory*; *Charlotte's Web*; *Frog and Toad Are Friends*; *James and the Giant Peach: A Children's Story*; *Leo the Late Bloomer*; *The Little Red Hen*; *Millions of Cats*; *Who's in Rabbit's House? A Masai Tale*; *Why Mosquitoes Buzz in People's Ears: A West African Tale*; or any favorite book featuring a variety of characters that can be represented by using high and low voices.

Directions:
While reading one or more of the above books to a child, assign high and low voices to the characters by varying the pitch (highness and lowness) of your own voice. After reading the book, discuss what made the characters sound interesting. Ask children to imitate the ways in which the various characters sounded. This is excellent preparation for Activities 14 and 15.

14. LISTENING TO HIGH SOUNDS AND LOW SOUNDS IN THE ENVIRONMENT

Directions:
Listen to sounds in the environment. Ask children to name as many sounds as possible while telling you if they are high or low.

Although no longer in print, the book *High Sounds, Low Sounds* by Franklyn M. Branley explains the principles of sound production through simple experiments. It may be possible to obtain a copy at your local library.

15. LOCATING HIGH AND LOW SOUNDS ON A KEYBOARD OR BARRED INSTRUMENT

Materials:
A piano, keyboard, or barred instrument.

Directions:
Have children explore the different sounds that can be produced on a piano, keyboard, or barred instrument. Next, see if they can identify which keys are high, which ones are low, and which are in the middle.

Help children discover that high tones are on the right-hand side and low tones are on the left. Illustrate that the bars on xylophones or other such instruments are of different lengths. See if they can discover that the high bars are short and the low bars are long. Point out the comparison that high instruments (violins and piccolos) are short whereas low instruments (tubas and basses) are long.

Variations:
An older child can demonstrate high sounds and low sounds on an instrument that he/she plays. Have children guess which sounds are high and which are low. *The Trumpet of the Swan* could be read, and a trumpet player could demonstrate how one can change the pitch with one's lips and one's fingers. Demonstrations such as this add extra excitement to the music lesson.

Another option is to have children listen to a recording that features a variety of musical selections and therefore a variety of pitches (such as the recording listed below).

Suggested musical resources:
Book: *The Trumpet of the Swan*. Recording: *Invitation to Music*.

16. USING BODY MOVEMENTS TO MATCH A MELODY

Directions:
Select a song with which children are familiar (see the listing below). You may want to select a song that deals with the same subject as one of the stories from Activity 13. For example, the song "I Had a Cat" can be learned in conjunction with the reading of *Millions of Cats*. As children sing or listen to the song, lead them in moving up and down in place, illustrating the shape of the melody. It is wise to select a piece of music that does not vary in regard to dynamics (loud and soft sounds). Otherwise, children may be responding to the dynamics rather than the melody. Point out that their bodies may at times move in patterns to accompany the melodic patterns (repetitive combinations of high and low notes) that may be present.

Variation:
If you're doing this activity with a group of children, have them illustrate the melodic contour of the song by each assuming a different position to represent a tone of the melody. For example, the child who is pretending to be the lowest tone can lie on the floor while the child who represents the highest tone can stand on tiptoe. Line children up so there is a visual representation of the melody as you sing the song together. Be sure to point out any melodic patterns that occur.

Suggested musical resources:
Song collections: *All Night, All Day: A Child's First Book of African-American Spirituals*; *American Folk Songs for Children in Home, School, and Nursery School: A Book for Children, Parents, and Teachers*; *Do Your Ears Hang Low? Fifty More Musical Fingerplays*; *Eye Winker, Tom Tinker, Chin Chopper: Fifty Musical Fingerplays*; *Go In and Out the Window: An Illustrated Songbook for Young People*; *The Raffi Singable Songbook*; *Singing Bee: A Collection of Favorite Children's Songs*. Recordings: *American Folk Songs for*

Children; *Baby Beluga*; *Corner Grocery Store and Other Singable Songs*; *Rise and Shine*; *Singable Songs for the Very Young*.

17. CREATING ORIGINAL STORIES AND IMPROVISING VOICES FOR THE CHARACTERS

Materials:

Original stories that the children have written.

Directions:

After completing one or more of the activities in this section, have children write stories that include a variety of characters. Younger children can dictate their stories to an adult. Read the stories through, and have children repeat lines from the stories using improvised voices to represent the characters they have created. Make sure they vary the sounds of their characters by using low and high voices.

CHAPTER THREE

Activities that Focus on the Elements of Dynamics and Tempo

I N THIS CHAPTER, CHILDREN CAN CONTINUE TO EXPLORE MUSI-cal elements by taking part in activities that incorporate some basic information about dynamics and tempo.

• *Dynamics*

There are loud sounds and quiet sounds (known as soft sounds), as well as various levels in between. Dynamic changes in music may occur gradually or abruptly.

• *Tempo*

There is fast music, slow music, and various levels in between. Tempo changes may occur gradually or abruptly.

THE ELEMENT OF DYNAMICS

IN THIS SECTION, CHILDREN WILL DISCOVER NOT ONLY THAT there is a wide range of dynamic levels but also that dynamics may change gradually or abruptly. One of the best ways of explaining dynamics is to actually demonstrate them during your introduction. Use a whispering voice while explaining the term *soft*, and use a loud voice while introducing the other extreme.

Notice that I said to use a loud voice. I did not say a shouting voice. I once watched a teacher attempting to get a group of second graders to sing louder for a musical they were scheduled to perform. He explained that what he wanted was the effect of a crowd shouting. Well, that's exactly what he got! It took four additional rehearsals before the children stopped using shouting voices and started using good, quality singing voices. This story illustrates the importance of presenting new material in an effective manner.

Activities 18 through 20 are designed to introduce children to the element of dynamics. Youngsters will learn about vocal dynamics that can be applied when reading stories; they will move their bodies to correspond with the dynamics encountered in examples of music; and they will play and conduct loud and soft sounds.

18. COMBINING CHILDREN'S LITERATURE WITH DYNAMICS

General literature for children:
Goodnight Moon; *Too Much Noise*; *Where the Wild Things Are: 25th Anniversary Edition*; *Why Mosquitoes Buzz in People's Ears: A West African Tale*; or any other books through which dynamics may be illustrated by varying the volume of one's voice while reading.

Directions:
While reading one or more of the above books to children, alter the dynamics by changing the volume of your voice. Be careful that you do not vary anything else, such as the pitch. Ask what it was that helped make the story exciting. Next, discuss various sounds that might be heard if you were a character in the book. Ask which of these sounds are loud and which are soft. Ask children to imagine if the characters

in the story have loud or soft voices. The children's work in this activity will lay the foundation for Activities 19 and 20.

Variation:

Select a brief passage from the story and read it several times, applying a different dynamic level with each reading. Ask your young listeners which way best fits the character of the story and why. If using *Goodnight Moon*, for example, children might suggest that a soft voice is appropriate since the rabbit in the story is attempting to fall asleep.

19. *ILLUSTRATING DYNAMICS WITH MOVEMENT*

Materials:

Any recordings that feature various levels of dynamics (see below).

Directions:

Play two or more selections that are different in dynamics, and have children respond to the music. Encourage kids to create big movements for loud songs like marches and smaller movements for soft selections such as lullabies. Children should also be exposed to music that starts at one dynamic level and changes to another. Try involving children with music that has gradual changes, as well as abrupt changes. Do this by changing the volume on your record or cassette player. Alter the dynamics in a variety of ways by changing the volume either suddenly or gradually.

Suggested musical resources:

Recordings: *Follow the Sunset: A Beginning Geography Record with Nine Songs from Around the World*; *Lullabies from 'Round the World*; *Play Your Instruments and Make a Pretty Sound*.

20. *PLAYING AND CONDUCTING DYNAMICS*

Materials:

The instruments that the children created in Activity 4.

Directions:

Have children demonstrate different levels of dynamics on the rhythm instruments they constructed in Activity 4. Ask them to play very soft, soft, loud, and very loud. Then see if they can start softly and gradually get louder (crescendo) and vice versa (decrescendo).

It's fun to play a game where one child is the conductor. As the child slowly raises his or her hands, the other children play louder. As the conductor slowly lowers his or her hands, the group gradually plays softer. Now have the conductor raise and lower his or her hands abruptly, so the children are playing sudden dynamic changes.

Variation:

Have children play along with the recordings from Activity 19. Tell them to play softly during songs like lullabies and loudly during lively selections. Combine their movements from Activity 19 with the playing of instruments. They can play loudly when marching and softly when tiptoeing.

THE ELEMENT OF TEMPO

I OFTEN PLAY A GAME WITH MY PRESCHOOL STUDENTS WHERE they must move at the proper speed to a piano accompaniment that I provide. As I constantly change the tempo, they excitedly change the rate of speed at which they walk, skip, gallop, or sink to the ground.

Using movement to teach about tempo can also be effective when children's stories are incorporated into the activity. Children can examine the rate of speed at which storybook characters might move or speak. They can also listen to a musical story and then move in the fashion of the characters portrayed.

21. USING CHILDREN'S LITERATURE TO INTRODUCE TEMPO

General literature for children:

Charlie and the Chocolate Factory; Charlotte's Web; Danny, the Champion of the World; Frog and Toad Are Friends; The New Kid on the Block; The Very Hungry Caterpillar; or any other book through which one may illustrate speed by altering the rate at which one reads.

Directions:

While reading one of the books listed, alter your voice so that it corresponds with how the characters might move. If reading *The Very Hungry Caterpillar,* for example, you might read the story very slowly. After you are finished, discuss how each of the characters moved: fast, slow, got faster, got slower, and so on.

Next, have children imagine they are a character from the book, and ask them to demonstrate how they might move or speak. Children will find great fun in this role-playing. Reinforce their actions with such statements as "My, you move quickly!" or "You're moving so slowly!"

Variation:

Older children may enjoy creating an entire play based on the book. Again point out that the characters should move appropriately.

22. LISTENING FOR TEMPI IN MUSICAL RECORDINGS

Materials:

A recording of *Peter and the Wolf* or *Carnival of the Animals* (various recordings of these selections are available through your public library).

Directions:

After children have visualized and acted out the movements of storybook characters, listen to a recording of *Peter and the Wolf* or *Carnival of the Animals.* Talk with your young listeners about how the different uses of tempi create mental pictures of the different characters in this story, and also discuss how they might move.

Listen to the recording again, and have children act out the story to the music. Make sure you stress that their actions coincide with the tempi encountered. The child who is pretending to be the grandfather, for example, should move slowly, whereas the one pretending to be the bird should move quickly.

Variation:

Put on a favorite recording, and have children move freely to the music. Reinforce the concept of tempo by pointing out when the music is slow, fast, speeding up, or slowing down.

CHAPTER FOUR

Activities for Teaching Timbre, Texture, and Harmony

T HE ACTIVITIES IN THIS CHAPTER FOCUS ON THE ELEMENTS OF timbre, texture, and harmony. In regard to timbre, children explore the unique qualities of their own voices. They learn that every instrument also has its own special sound. As the elements of texture and harmony are unfolded, children experience the beauty and enjoyment of blending one voice (be it human or instrumental) with another. Young musicians will come away with a basic understanding of these three important concepts:

- ● *Timbre*
  There is a difference between the speaking voice and the singing voice, and each individual has a unique voice. Musical instruments also have unique voices and are grouped by families based on similar characteristics.

- ● *Texture*
  Music can be made up of any number of instrumental or human voices, and this number in turn produces a thin or thick effect of sound.

- ● *Harmony*
  The combination of two or more tones performed together produces an effect known as harmony.

THE ELEMENT OF TIMBRE

THROUGH THE FOLLOWING ACTIVITIES, CHILDREN WILL DISCOVER that everyone and every instrument has a characteristic voice. Since children take great pride in knowing they are special, they should be delighted to learn that even their voices are unique.

You will first play a game with the children that illustrates the difference between a singing voice and a speaking voice. Then you'll play different rhythm instruments for them; they should close their eyes and identify each instrument as it is played. Children will learn that orchestral instruments are grouped by families. Finally, they will use children's literature and recordings in a study of the symphony orchestra, focusing their attention on the characteristic sound of each instrument heard.

23. *GUESSING WHO SPOKE OR SANG*

General literature for children:
Any favorite story.

Directions:
This activity works best if done with a group. Tell children that they are to close their eyes and that you will be tapping one of them on the shoulder. Whoever is tapped is to say the word *hello*. The other children must then guess which person spoke. Each time a correct answer is given, ask the question, "How did you know who it was that spoke?" The answer will inevitably be "By his [or her] voice!" Keep repeating the point that every person has his or her own special speaking voice.

On the following day or session, play the game again, having the children *sing* the hello. What notes they sing does not matter at this point, as long as they are singing and not speaking. As you play the game, stress the idea that each person's singing voice is unique.

Remember that very young children may have difficulty understanding the difference between a speaking voice and a singing voice and may have trouble producing one or the other when asked to do so. Be sure to give them encouragement and constant praise.

Next, have children select a character from a favorite story. Ask them: How might this character speak? How would this character sing? This exercise will lay the foundation for the next activities in this section.

Variation:

After children are confident in their knowledge of the distinction between a singing voice and a speaking voice and are able to demonstrate each with ease, allow them to choose how they wish to produce the hello. Some may choose to sing, while others may choose to speak.

Variation:

For added fun, have children disguise their voices. Point out the fact that instruments can also have their voices disguised. The trumpet, for example, can be made to sound differently with the addition of a mute (an object placed inside the bell of the instrument). This is the perfect introduction to the next activity, which illustrates that each instrument also has its own unique tone color.

24. GUESSING THE RHYTHM INSTRUMENT

Materials:

Rhythm instruments or handmade instruments.

Directions:

To prepare for this activity, encourage children to experiment with various rhythm instruments in order to become familiar with their sounds. Ask children to close their eyes while you play each rhythm instrument, and have them guess which was played. Point out that although each was unique in sound, some may have sounded similar to one another. This is an excellent introduction to Activity 25.

25. GROUPING ORCHESTRAL INSTRUMENTS BY FAMILIES

Directions:

Collect pictures of orchestral instruments from old magazines and glue them onto three-by-five cards. Ask children if they sound like a family member (brother, sister, father, or mother). Tell them that although they may sound like someone else in their family, they still have a unique voice as was illustrated in Activity 23. Reinforce the idea that this is true of instruments as well. Next group the pictures of the instruments according to family (percussion family, string family, woodwind family, and brass family). Then shuffle the pictures and have the children attempt to correctly group them.

Discuss the fact that while orchestral instruments each have a special voice, they are grouped by families on the basis of certain similarities: in sound, in the way they are played, and in the material from which they are made. The glossary of musical terms defines the orchestral families.

26. COMBINING CHILDREN'S LITERATURE WITH AN INTRODUCTION TO THE SYMPHONY ORCHESTRA

Materials:

Pictures of orchestral instruments, as well as the books listed below.

Directions:

Listen to a recording of *Peter and the Wolf* or *The Young Person's Guide to the Orchestra* (various recordings of these selections should be obtainable through your public library system), each of which provides descriptive introductions to select orchestral instruments. As the various instruments are introduced on the recording, show pictures of the same instruments (using the picture cards you prepared for Activity 25) and discuss their sounds. After children have listened to *Peter and the Wolf*, ask them to draw a picture of a favorite character and of the instrument that was used to represent that character.

Next, read the book *Peter and the Wolf*, so kids can see how a professional illustrator imagined the characters to appear. Finally, read the book *The Philharmonic Gets Dressed* for a fun look at a symphony orchestra.

Variation:

Listen to music that features electronic instruments or instruments from various countries. Then show pictures of the instruments represented, and have children draw a picture of his or her favorite instrument. Ask a child to tell you why it is a favorite. Try to select recordings that allow your young listeners to hear one instrument clearly at a time.

If using examples of music other than orchestral, you will find that it is now necessary to use broader terms when categorizing instruments. For example, a sitar from India would not be found in the string family of a Western symphony orchestra, but it does possess strings. At this point, children can be introduced to additional terms for classifying instruments: idiophone, membranophone, aerophone, chordophone, and electronic instruments (see the Glossary of Musical Terms for definitions of these terms).

Suggested musical resources:

Books: *Peter and the Wolf*; *The Philharmonic Gets Dressed*.

THE ELEMENT OF TEXTURE

ONCE CHILDREN REALIZE THAT EACH INSTRUMENT AND HUMAN voice has its own special sound, they should be made aware that instruments and voices can be combined in different numbers to create thin and thick textures. This point can be easily conveyed through the use of children's literature.

27. *INTEGRATING CHILDREN'S BOOKS WITH THE STUDY OF TEXTURE*

General literature for children:

Any books from the Annotated Bibliography of General Literature for Children can be used in conjunction with this activity.

Directions:

Read two books to children that vary from each other in terms of the number of characters. Discuss how books with a narrator or one character produce a different mood or feeling than books with two or more characters. Ask a child to describe how it sounds in the classroom or at home when there is one person speaking, two speaking, three, and so forth.

Now play two or more selections of music. Each should have a different number of instruments and therefore a different type of texture. To describe the different textures, use such words as *thin* or *thick*, *light* or *heavy*.

Finally, have children choose a musical selection that would best serve as background music for the literature read as part of this activity (see recordings listed below). A musical selection featuring a solo instrument, for example, might serve as an appropriate background for a book that features one character. And a duet might be selected for a story that involves two characters.

Suggested musical resources:

Recordings: *Invitation to Music*; *Play Your Instruments and Make a Pretty Sound*.

28. *CREATING SOUND EFFECTS TO PRODUCE A TEXTURED STORY*

General literature for children:

Any story in which earlier portions are repeated each time something new is introduced—a cumulative story (see the Subject Guide for examples).

Directions:

Read a cumulative story to children. Then assign repetitive words or sound effects which the kids are to perform every time a word cue is heard in the story. For example, every time the word *cat* is heard, a child might say "Meow, meow, meow, meow."

If doing this activity at home, you may first wish to make a tape recording of the story. Both you and your child can then accompany the tape with vocal sound effects to produce a layered texture. If doing this activity with a class, you can involve several groups, each of which will enter at different times and with different sound effects. Children will find that this approach creates layers of varying degrees as groups enter and reenter. Discuss the effect that this has on the listener.

THE ELEMENT OF HARMONY

ONCE CHILDREN UNDERSTAND THAT VOICES AND INSTRUMENTS can be combined to form varying textures, they are ready to learn about the joining of two or more voices to create the effect known as harmony.

The activities that follow will involve children in the recitation of poems as rounds in order to create spoken harmony. They can experiment further by adding *ostinati* to accompany these spoken rounds. They will then progress to the singing and composing of rounds and ostinati (see the Glossary of Musical Terms for definitions).

29. USING CHILDREN'S BOOKS TO CREATE SPOKEN ROUNDS

General literature for children:
One or more poems from any of these books: *Charlie and the Chocolate Factory*; *It's Halloween*; *James and the Giant Peach: A Children's Story*; *The New Kid on the Block*; *The Random House Book of Mother Goose: A Treasury of 306 Timeless Nursery Rhymes*; *Sing a Song of Popcorn: Every Child's Book of Poems*; or *The Sky Is Full of Song*.

Directions:
Begin by explaining the concept of a round. Next, play a recording of various rounds (see recording listed below). See if children can detect the entrance of each new part. You may wish to have them raise their hands each time they hear a new part enter.

Next, read a poem aloud from one of the above books. Go over the poem several times until the children have it memorized and can recite it. This process may take a few minutes or a few days, depending on the age of the children and the complexity of the poem.

Now see if children can perform the poem again as a spoken round. If working with a class, assign one group of children to begin the poem. The second group of children will enter when the first group has reached the second line. (Parents working with only one child will find it useful to record the poem as an initial step. The tape can then take the place of the first part, and you and your child can act as the second.)

Suggested musical resource:
Recording: *Wee Sing Sing-Alongs*.

30. RECITING SPOKEN ROUNDS WITH THE ADDITION OF OSTINATI

General literature for children:
Any of the books from Activity 29.

Directions:

Have children memorize a poem as described in the preceding activity. Explain the concept of an ostinato. Then have one group of children recite the poem, while another group recites an ostinato (a line that repeats over and over again). The ostinato may be a line that they have created, the title of the poem, or a selected line from the poem.

When children have mastered the last two activities, break the class into three groups. Two groups will perform the poem as a spoken round while the third group performs the ostinato.

31. SINGING ROUNDS

Materials:

A recording of various rounds (see recording listed below).

Directions:

Now that children have taken part in the production of spoken harmony, the next step is to have them *sing* rounds and ostinati. As preparation, they can try singing along with a tape that features rounds. Have the voices on the tape act as the first part while you and the kids sing the second. Once children can sing a number of rounds along with a recording, they are ready to sing on their own. Have them create a movement for each line of the round and perform these movements while they are singing. This will help them keep track of where they are without becoming confused.

If children have difficulty, it can sometimes be helpful to begin by having each group sing only one line from the round over and over again. After each group knows their one line, have all the groups sing their parts simultaneously.

Variation:

Sing rounds that are on the same subject as the literature they have been reading (see song collections below).

Suggested musical resources:
Recording: *Wee Sing Sing-Alongs.* Song collections: *American Folk Songs for Children in Home, School, and Nursery School: A Book for Children, Parents, and Teachers*; *Do Your Ears Hang Low? Fifty More Musical Fingerplays*; *Eye Winker, Tom Tinker, Chin Chopper: Fifty Musical Fingerplays*; *Go In and Out the Window: An Illustrated Songbook for Young People*; *The Raffi Singable Songbook*; *Singing Bee: A Collection of Favorite Children's Songs.*

32. COMPOSING ROUNDS AND OSTINATI

Directions:
As a final activity, have children write their own poems and sing them to tunes of traditional rounds. They are to create movements for each line of the round as well. Experiment with the addition of vocal ostinati. A poem dealing with the ocean will literally come to life when ostinati are added that sound like waves as they hit the shore ("boooooom, crash, boooooom, crash") or delicately caress the sand ("shh, shh, swissssh").

CHAPTER FIVE

Activities that Introduce the Element of Form and Musical Notation as a Means of Communication

I N THIS CHAPTER, LET'S LOOK AT THE ELEMENT OF FORM AND the necessity of musical notation (written symbols). The activities in this chapter are designed to promote an increased awareness of:

- **Form**
Compositions may contain melodic and rhythmic patterns that recur; lines (phrases) in a composition may be like or unlike; and larger sections in a musical selection may be similar or contrasting.

- **Notation**
Music may be notated (written down), and this notation communicates meaning.

AS YOU READ THROUGH VARIOUS BOOKS, YOU MAY HAVE DISCOV-
ered words, lines, or even major sections of a story or poem
that were recurring. Authors often use contrasting material
for variety and repetition to produce a sense of unity. This is
true of composers as well.

Compositions may contain repetitive patterns, like and unlike phrases, and major sections that are the same or different. As similar and contrasting material is used, the work
takes on a characteristic shape or *form*. This form in turn af-
fects the listener.

'The next three activities introduce children to the element
of form in both music and literature. Activities 33 and 34 deal
with the structure of various stories, poems, and musical selections. In Activity 35 children create a picture book that illustrates the form of a favorite song.

33. COMBINING LITERATURE WITH THE STUDY OF MUSICAL FORM

General literature for children:

Brown Bear, Brown Bear, What Do You See?; *Caps for Sale:
A Tale of a Peddler, Some Monkeys, and Their Monkey Busi-
ness*; *Chickens Aren't the Only Ones*; *Millions of Cats*; *Too
Much Noise*; *The Very Hungry Caterpillar*; *Who's in Rabbit's
House? A Masai Tale*; or any other books that feature repe-
tition or cumulation.

Directions:

Read one or more of the above stories to children, and emphasize the fact that certain words or portions of the work
recur while others do not.

Now select a favorite song (see song collections and recordings listed below), and listen for melodic and/or rhythmic
patterns that are repetitive. Are there lines (phrases)

within the song that are the same, slightly different, completely different? Are there major sections that are similar or contrasting? Conclude your discussion by reinforcing the idea that musical elements may be arranged in a variety of ways and that the structure or form of a composition is the outcome of this arrangement. This activity will prepare children for Activity 34.

Suggested musical resources:

Song collections: *All Night, All Day: A Child's First Book of African-American Spirituals*; *American Folk Songs for Children in Home, School, and Nursery School: A Book for Children, Parents, and Teachers*; *Do Your Ears Hang Low? Fifty More Musical Fingerplays*; *Eye Winker, Tom Tinker, Chin Chopper: Fifty Musical Fingerplays*; *Go In and Out the Window: An Illustrated Songbook for Young People*; *The Raffi Singable Songbook*; *Singing Bee: A Collection of Favorite Children's Songs*. Recordings: *American Folk Songs for Children*; *Baby Beluga*; *Corner Grocery Store and Other Singable Songs*; *Rise and Shine*; *Singable Songs for the Very Young*.

34. USING RIGHT HANDS AND LEFT HANDS TO ILLUSTRATE PHRASES

Materials:

The recordings listed below, chalk, and a chalkboard.

Directions:

Play a variety of musical selections. While doing so, point out repetitive patterns, like and unlike phrases, and similar and contrasting sections. Next, select a new piece for discussion, and tell children that they will be concentrating on the identification of like and unlike phrases.

Ask children to raise their right hands when they hear the first line (phrase). Label this line *A*, and draw a picture on the chalkboard of an object that begins with the letter *A*. Have children raise the same hand if the next line is similar, and draw another *A* object on the board. If the line is different, have the children raise their left hands, and be sure to draw an item on the board that begins with the letter *B*.

Continue your examination of the song until there is a complete pictorial representation of the phrases. Sing through the song again, having the children raise appropriate hands while you point to the symbols you have drawn. Occasionally, when there are more than two options, children may need to participate with partners.

"Mary Had a Little Lamb" is an example of this.

> *Mary Had a Little Lamb,*
> *Little Lamb, Little Lamb,*
> *Mary Had a Little Lamb,*
> *With Fleece as White as Snow.*

This song would be illustrated as follows:

- Label the first line *A*, and draw an airplane on the board. Have the first child raise his or her right hand.
- Since the second line is different, draw a picture of a boat and write the letter *B*. Have the first child raise his or her left hand.
- Label the third line *A* since it is identical to the first line, and draw an airplane. The first child will now raise his or her right hand again.
- Label the fourth line *C*, and draw a car. Now the second child will need to raise a hand.

Tell children that this song can be said to be in ABAC form. Continue to give the children songs with more complex forms.

Variations:

You may wish to play this game again while focusing on larger sections of a song, rather than on each line. A verse, for example, can be referred to as the "A section," whereas the refrain can be identified as the "B section."

Older children may enjoy listening for melodic and rhythmic patterns that recur and creating body movements or hand motions to represent these patterns. Take note, however, that this requires a more attentive ear and quite possibly a number of practice sessions.

Another variation is to try this activity with a favorite poem or story.

Suggested musical resources:
Recordings: *Baby Beluga*; *Corner Grocery Store and Other Singable Songs*; *Rise and Shine*.

35. CREATING BOOKS BASED ON THE FORMS OF SONGS

Materials:
Items for creating books such as paper, felt pens, crayons, and brads; as well as a children's story based on a folk song, children's song, or patriotic song (see below for suggestions).

Directions:
Begin by reading a book that is based on a song. Now sing the song on which the book is based (the Annotated Bibliography of Musical Literature for Children includes information on which books contain melodies).

Do certain words repeat and therefore create patterns? Are there lines or sections that are the same or different? Ask children how this form is illustrated in the story.

Next, have children illustrate the phrases of a favorite song by creating their own books. Instruct children to draw a picture for each line of the song. If there is a line that recurs, they will need to draw the same picture each time it does so. They will need to draw different pictures for lines that are contrasting. The final product will be an illustrated example of the song's form.

If doing this activity at home, share the books by making them part of the family reading time (at bedtime, etc.). If the activity is done at school, share the books and songs with another class.

Suggested musical resources:
Picture books based on songs: *Drummer Hoff*; *Follow the Drinking Gourd*; *Frog Went A-Courtin'*; *I Know an Old Lady Who Swallowed a Fly*; *The Little Drummer Boy*; *Mommy,*

Buy Me a China Doll; *Old MacDonald Had a Farm*; *Six Little Ducks*; *Skip to My Lou*; *The Star-Spangled Banner*; *Yankee Doodle*. (It should be noted that many more books of this genre exist.)

INTRODUCTION TO MUSICAL NOTATION

UNDOUBTEDLY, CHILDREN WILL BE EAGER BY NOW TO BEGIN looking at written music. Once a piece of music is placed in front of them, their questions will be unceasing. If you do not read music, you may at first feel overwhelmed. But it's perfectly acceptable to begin by simply telling children that there are symbols for everything they have discussed thus far. There are signs for high and low sounds, long and short sounds, loud and soft sounds, and more.

Young musicians should then be introduced to the fact that music is a form of communication since it allows us to express ideas and emotions. Children should finally be given the opportunity to create their own musical symbols.

The following activities illustrate how these concepts may be included at home or in the classroom. If children will be studying music reading in the near future, the suggested activities will also serve nicely as an introduction to this process.

36. COMPARING MUSICAL SYMBOLS WITH WRITTEN LANGUAGE

General literature for children:
Any of the books from the Annotated Bibliography of Musical Literature for Children.

Materials:

A number of written samples of music.

Directions:

Introduce children to various examples of musical notation. Try to include samples of vocal music, piano music, and more. Explain why various symbols in music are needed (to convey whether the notes are to be played long, short, high, low, etc.).

Next, read to children a book selected from the Annotated Bibliography of Musical Literature for Children. Discuss the importance of symbols in our written language (letters when combined create words; punctuation gives meaning to a sentence; etc.). In so doing, discuss the fact that music can be thought of as a form of literature; music, like books, can express thoughts and emotions. Explain to children that musical symbols enable a composer to preserve these ideas and emotions so that a performer may duplicate them at a later date.

37. CREATING MUSICAL SYMBOLS

Materials:

Any favorite children's song (see song collections listed below).

Directions:

Begin by speaking the lyrics while clapping the rhythm. Decide where the long sounds, short sounds, and silences occur (you may wish to review Activity 9 before you begin). Ask children to invent their own symbols to represent the various sounds and silences. These symbols may be sticks, lines, shapes, or pictures of objects. Chant the lyrics again while pointing to the symbols. Ask whether this system communicates all possible musical elements or if there are others that are not represented, such as the melody.

Now sing the melody and have children decide how to represent high and low sounds in addition to the rhythm. They may want to simply place their initial symbols in high and

low positions to illustrate the contour of the melodic line.
Ask if the picture addresses tempo and dynamics. If not,
have children create symbols for these as well. When completed, sing the song together while pointing to the symbols.

Suggested musical resources:

Song collections: *All Night, All Day: A Child's First Book of
African-American Spirituals*; *American Folk Songs for Chil-
dren in Home, School, and Nursery School: A Book for Chil-
dren, Parents, and Teachers*; *Do Your Ears Hang Low? Fifty
More Musical Fingerplays*; *Eye Winker, Tom Tinker, Chin
Chopper: Fifty Musical Fingerplays*; *Go In and Out the Win-
dow: An Illustrated Songbook for Young People*; *The Raffi
Singable Songbook*; *Singing Bee: A Collection of Favorite
Children's Songs*.

CHAPTER SIX

Activities to Promote the Development of Musical Skills and Creativity

A S CHILDREN WERE INTRODUCED TO VARIOUS MUSICAL CON-cepts in Chapters 2 through 5, you may have noticed that they were also encouraged to sing, play instruments, move to music, listen to music, and begin to use self-devised, musical symbols to notate sounds.

This chapter will continue to support the development of such skills by encouraging children to act as performers, arrangers, composers, choreographers, and musicologists. Listed below are five skill areas and the means by which these will be enhanced.

• *Singing skills*
Children will sing with clear, relaxed voices and will feel at ease singing alone or with others. They will also create their own vocal arrangements based on favorite songs.

• *Instrumental skills*
Children will perform on a variety of instruments (rhythm, handmade, etc.) and will feel more at ease playing alone or with others. They will also create their own instrumental arrangements.

• *Movement skills*

Children will respond more freely and naturally to the mood and musical elements of a selection, and they will choreograph their own dances.

• *Reading and writing skills*

Children will compose their own songs, and use their own symbols to notate their creations.

• *Listening skills*

Children will listen to a composition and identify the musical elements heard by creating *sound drawings* (pictorial interpretations of the music).

Parents and teachers can continue to use children's books to accomplish all of these objectives.

ACTIVITIES FOR DEVELOPING SKILLS IN SINGING AND VOCAL ARRANGING

AS AN ADULT, HOW YOU PERSONALLY FEEL ABOUT YOUR VOICE OR about singing in public may be the direct result of the positive or negative feedback you experienced as a child. In order for individuals to feel confident about their voices when they reach adulthood, they must have positive, yet constructive, experiences during childhood. Children's singing activities should be joyful, creative, and allow for self-expression. From the beginning, however, children should also be introduced to good vocal techniques. Here are some ideas to keep in mind when working with children.

A child's voice should never sound as though it is being forced or strained in any way. Keep in mind that a voice that remains relaxed and unstressed will often be one that lasts longer as well. Encourage children to breathe deeply, use good posture, and enunciate clearly. Allow each child to develop his or her own special and beautiful sound. When children sing as a group, continue to emphasize these ideas while stressing the cooperation needed in order to create a beautiful, ensemble sound. Once children have developed good singing habits and they have sung in a variety of ensemble combinations, they will thoroughly enjoy creating and performing their own vocal arrangements.

You may wonder how an adult with little or no musical background can assist children in these endeavors. The following activities present a detailed plan for doing so.

38. CHORAL READING AS A PRELUDE TO SINGING AND VOCAL ARRANGING

General literature for children:

It's Halloween; *The New Kid on the Block*; *The Random House Book of Mother Goose: A Treasury of 306 Timeless Nursery Rhymes*; *Sing a Song of Popcorn: Every Child's Book of Poems*; *The Sky Is Full of Song*; or any other collections of poetry.

Directions:

Read to the children a poem selected from one of the above books. Enunciate the words clearly, and breathe at the ends of the lines, or what we refer to as *phrases*. Tell children that they will be performing the poem together (as a choral reading) and will be learning terms to describe various vocal combinations. Have children now recite the selection with you. Stress the need for them to breathe and enunciate in a similar fashion. Instruct the children that by speaking together, they are acting as a *chorus*.

Next, have youngsters participate in a variety of vocal ensembles. One person (*solo*) might read the first line, two people (*duet*) might read the second, three people (*trio*) might recite the third stanza, and four people (*quartet*) may finish up with the last line. Have children repeat the poem as an

entire group (*chorus*). By continuing to use such terms as
solo and *duet*, you are introducing children to vocabulary
that will be needed when they create their own arrangements.

On another occasion, select a favorite song with similar
subject matter as the poem that was just explored (see song
collections listed below). *Sing* the song together as a group,
and again refer to the class as a chorus. Then see if any of
the children would like to perform the selection as a solo, a
duet, a trio, and so on. Remember to continue to use this
terminology, and encourage those who volunteer to sing. Reinforce the characteristics of good-quality singing and the
importance of working together as a group.

Children may now complete a vocal arrangement as a
group project. They should select a song and decide how and
where they will use solo voices, duets, trios, a chorus, and
so on. Try to include all children in this activity. Ask them
what effect the various combinations have on the listener.
This project can be made to last over a period of several days.

This would be an excellent time to review and reinforce
the element of texture as introduced in Activities 27 and 28.

Suggested musical resources:
Song collections: *American Folk Songs for Children in
Home, School, and Nursery School: A Book for Children,
Parents, and Teachers*; *Go In and Out the Window: An Illus-
trated Songbook for Young People*; *The Raffi Singable Song-
book*; *Singing Bee! A Collection of Favorite Children's Songs*.

39. COMBINING RECORDINGS WITH VOCAL ARRANGING

Materials:
Recordings featuring a variety of vocal ensembles (see recordings listed below).

Directions:
Activity 38 serves nicely to prepare children for the following. Listen to as many different types of vocal arrangements
as possible, and see if kids can identify when they are hearing solo voices, duets, trios, choruses, and so forth.

Next, select a favorite song from the recording. When a solo voice is heard, have a child sing along with the selection. If the song features a duet, have two children sing. Try this exercise with a number of musical works. Then encourage strong, independent singing by having children perform the songs without the use of the recording. Continue to stress good vocal techniques (breathing, enunciating, etc.). You may also use the second side of *You'll Sing a Song and I'll Sing a Song*, which features instrumental accompaniments to the songs included on the first side.

As a final project, allow children to arrange the song differently from the way it was presented on the recording.

Variation:

This is a good time to take children to a performance that features various vocal ensembles. Afterward, discuss the types of ensembles heard.

Suggested musical resources:

Recordings: *Sing Children Sing: Songs of Mexico*; *Sing Children Sing: Songs of the United States of America*; *You'll Sing a Song and I'll Sing a Song*.

ACTIVITIES FOR DEVELOPING INSTRUMENTAL SKILLS (PLAYING AND ARRANGING)

YOU MAY HAVE NOTICED THAT CHILDREN THOROUGHLY ENJOY ACtivities involving musical instruments. Not only are children fascinated with the diverse sounds that can be created, they enjoy being given the opportunity to create such sounds. As they explore various sound sources, they also increase their understanding of musical elements.

Parents and teachers, therefore, need to provide supportive

environments that allow children the time to create, explore, and work cooperatively as budding musicians. In the activities that follow, the children can have fun creating instrumental sound effects to represent sounds mentioned in the stories. They will also read and write about musicians and create instrumental arrangements to accompany recordings.

Before doing these activities, children should already have had the opportunity to experiment with a variety of instruments: percussion instruments; autoharps; barred instruments (xylophones, glockenspiels, etc.); the piano; or even handmade instruments if others are not available. (It is suggested that Activities 4, 15, and 24 be completed first.)

40. INTEGRATING CHILDREN'S BOOKS WITH INSTRUMENTS

General literature for children:

Too Much Noise; *Who's in Rabbit's House? A Masai Tale*; *Why Mosquitoes Buzz in People's Ears: A West African Tale*; or other books for which instrumental sound effects can be created to represent a character or event in the story.

Directions:

After reading one of the books listed, decide what instrument would best represent a character or event in the book. You might try asking children such questions as: "What type of instrument could be used to represent raindrops?" "What type could be used to sound like a train, or a bird, or a frog?" Try to incorporate a variety of instruments. Have children create simple ostinati to represent the characters or events in the story.

Read the book or poem again, and allow children to perform their instrumental parts each time the corresponding event occurs or the character is mentioned. (If doing this activity at home, you and your child may each perform a separate instrumental part.)

Review Activity 28 and the use of vocal sound effects. Now read the story again, and see if children can combine vocal sound effects with instrumental sound effects.

41. READING AND WRITING ABOUT INSTRUMENTALISTS

Materials:

Picture books about instrumentalists (see below).

Directions:

Begin by reading to children a book that focuses on an instrumentalist or instrumental ensemble. Discuss the characters in the story and the part music plays in their lives.

Next, have a child pretend that he or she is a great musician. Ask the child such questions as: "What instrument do you play?" "What kind of music do you play?" "When did you start playing?" or "How do you feel when you perform?" Children who cannot yet write can dictate their stories to an adult.

Variation:

Introduce various musical professions by reading picture books about singers, conductors, choreographers, and more.

Suggested musical resources:

Books: *Ben's Trumpet*; *The Bremen-Town Musicians*; *Geraldine, the Music Mouse*; *Music, Music for Everyone*; *Pages of Music*; *The Philharmonic Gets Dressed*; *The Trumpet of the Swan*.

42. CREATING AN INSTRUMENTAL ARRANGEMENT TO ACCOMPANY A RECORDING

Materials:

Various musical instruments (rhythm, barred, handmade, etc.).

Directions:

Prepare children for this activity by having them first keep a steady beat (as clapped by an adult leader) with a percussion instrument or handmade instrument of their choice. Then play a selection from one of the recordings listed below, and have children keep the beat along with the recording.

Ask them if it sounds good to have all the instruments playing at one time. They may decide that they like the sound of this in some places but not in others. Now guide children through the process of arranging the song. Have them decide which instrument or combination of instruments will play during various sections of the piece.

Attending a performance that features a variety of ensemble combinations would be ideal at this point.

Suggested musical resources:
Recordings: *Play Your Instruments and Make a Pretty Sound*; *Rhythms of Childhood*; *You'll Sing a Song and I'll Sing a Song*.

ACTIVITIES FOR DEVELOPING MOVEMENT SKILLS

YOU MAY HAVE NOTICED IN PREVIOUS ACTIVITIES THAT AS CHILdren are introduced to musical facts, they are also consistently engaged in movement activities. They can perform fingerplays in Activity 11 and create large movements in Activity 12, to illustrate rhythm. They create motions to better understand harmony in Activities 31 and 32. Movement is also incorporated in Activities 16, 19, 20, 22, and 34 to explore the elements of melody, dynamics, tempo, and form.

As a teacher, I try to include movement in every class lesson. I will, at times, even introduce a movement game to my private students. Movement keeps the lesson alive and interesting. It also enables children to directly experience what is being discussed. And it's fun!

In this section, children will have the opportunity to act as choreographers. They will listen to a recording (instrumental only) and select a book that matches the mood of the recording. They can then create a dance based on both the recording and the book. After this, they will be ready to each create an original dance based on a folk song.

43. USING CHILDREN'S BOOKS AS AN AID TO CHOREOGRAPHY

General literature for children:
Any favorite picture book, as well as a recording that matches the mood or actions discussed in the story (see recordings listed below).

Directions:
Play a recording (instrumental only) for children, and then discuss the music. Does it sound happy or sad? Does it make you think of birds, animals, the ocean? Now read aloud a book that suits the mood or style of the recording. Ask children to pretend they are a character from the story. Tell them that they will now be creating a dance that represents the character's actions.

If, for example, children say that the music makes them think of animals scurrying, you may decide to read *The Little Red Hen*. Children may create movements to represent the hen going to the mill, grounding the flour, baking the bread, feeding her children, and so on. These movements can then be combined to create a dance. The recording used earlier may be used as an accompaniment to the dance.

Suggested musical resources:
Recordings: *Invitation to Music*; *You'll Sing a Song and I'll Sing a Song* (second side is instrumental only).

44. CREATING A DANCE BASED ON A FOLK SONG

Materials:
Any favorite folk song and the books and recordings listed below.

Directions:

After the children have completed Activity 43, they are ready to create their own dance based on a folk song. Have them select a favorite folk song (see song collection and recording listed below). Ask them to create a motion for the first line of the song, another for the second line, and so on. These should be full motions involving arms and feet (skipping, swinging partners, etc.). When completed, sing the song and perform the dance at the same time.

After some practice, you will be excited to see children naturally begin to emphasize various musical elements, including form, beat, rhythm, and melody. Encourage these responses.

For a fun conclusion, you may wish to read picture books that illustrate the characters in dance (see below).

Suggested musical resources:

Picture books on dance: *Barn Dance!*; *Max*; *Song and Dance Man*. Song collection: *American Folk Songs for Children in Home, School, and Nursery School: A Book for Children, Parents, and Teachers*. Recording: *American Folk Songs for Children*.

LAYING THE FOUNDATION FOR READING, WRITING, AND COMPOSING

ONE OF THE MOST JOYFUL THINGS TO HEAR IS THE CHILD WHO says, "Listen, I made up a song!" As a music teacher, I believe we should treat this creation with the same respect that we give to a child's art project or original story. Encourage such creativity, and it will occur again and again. To preserve the event, many parents record their children's compositions with tape players, camcorders, and the like. Those who have backgrounds in music write the songs down and begin to teach their children how to read the traditional musical symbols. Children take great pride, however, in inscribing their songs themselves. The musical symbols from Activity 37 should enable them to do so.

In the next activity, they will in fact use these symbols to notate original compositions. They will also be introduced to stories about composers, both real and imaginary.

45. USING POETRY AS AN AID IN COMPOSING

General literature for children:

It's Halloween; *The New Kid on the Block*; *The Random House Book of Mother Goose: A Treasury of 306 Timeless Nursery Rhymes*; *Sing a Song of Popcorn: Every Child's Book of Poems*; *The Sky Is Full of Song*; or any other collections of poetry.

Directions:

Select a favorite poem, and tell children that together you will be transforming the poem into a song. Inform them that you will be using the notation created in Activity 37.

Write the words of the poem down, and recite it together. Next, use the symbols developed to notate the rhythm. Create a melody for the poem (a xylophone or piano may be of assistance), and have children use their symbols to notate the contour of the melody. Make sure they place symbols on the page to represent the dynamics and the tempo.

After children have successfully completed a song, a final project might be to create their own original lyrics and melodies and notate their pieces using their own symbols. Make copies of each composition to make it easier for children to teach their class members the songs they have created.

As a follow-up activity, read stories to children that focus on various composers (see books listed below).

Suggested musical resources:
Books on composers: *America, I Hear You: A Story About George Gershwin*; *Beethoven*; *Wolferl: The First Six Years in the Life of Wolfgang Amadeus Mozart, 1756–1762*; *Women Music Makers*.

AN ACTIVITY TO STRENGTHEN LISTENING SKILLS

TO BE SUCCESSFUL IN SCHOOL AND IN LIFE IN GENERAL, IT IS ES-sential that children develop good listening skills. Taking part in musical activities is a wonderful and enjoyable way of encouraging children to listen carefully. The next project requires the children to listen attentively to a selection and then to act as musicologists by interpreting the music. They can do this by drawing a picture of what they think the music is about. Children should be encouraged to discuss specific musical elements that prompted their answers.

In one of my preschool classes, I played Pachelbel's *Canon in D Major* for a group of four- and five-year-old children. It was rewarding to hear their responses to the question "What is this music about?" One said it made her think of a whale swimming in the ocean; another said the music was about her cat purring; still another said the music was about a forest. Their drawings, needless to say, were exquisite.

46. DRAWING A PICTURE OF WHAT THE MUSIC IS ABOUT

Materials:
Paper, pencils, and crayons; the recording and book listed below; as well as another favorite picture book.

Directions:

Read the book *Rondo in C*, which features a little girl playing for a recital and illustrates what the audience is thinking as she plays. Discuss how the music may cause one to think of images.

Now play a musical selection. Have children draw a picture of items or events that came to mind. In this initial step, have them create black-and-white drawings only.

Next, play the selection again, and ask children what colors they imagine. Allow kids the opportunity to fill in their drawings with colors. Discuss what musical elements prompted these answers. Is red the color of choice because the music is loud? Do they choose pink because the music is soft? Encourage them to use musical terminology when discussing their pictures.

Select any favorite picture book with beautiful illustrations. Ask children to imagine it without pictures. Present the analogy that just as an artist brings paintings to life with color and line and the use of texture, a composer uses musical elements to bring life to a composition.

Suggested musical resources:

Book: *Rondo in C*. Recording: *Invitation to Music*.

CHAPTER SEVEN

Activities for Examining America's Musical Heritage

C HILDREN OF THE UNITED STATES HAVE INHERITED AN EXCIT-ing and inspiring repertoire of music. In our country to-day, one can find examples of music not only from various time periods but from a variety of cultures as well. Children should get to know the range of our heritage when selecting music to sing, play, or for listening.

By participating in these activities, children will learn that:

- music has significance within a culture—it communi-cates ideas, information, and emotions;
- music may be influenced by a society's heritage and history;
- music from many cultural groups may be found throughout America today.

THE SIGNIFICANCE OF MUSIC

SOMETIMES WE FAIL TO REALIZE JUST HOW GREAT A PART MUSIC plays in our lives. If we pause a moment and listen, we will find that we hear it wherever we go. Music is used, and has been used over the years, to tell others what we are thinking and feeling. It is a significant part of our lives. In this section, the children will explore how often music is heard during the course of the day. By looking at picture books based on songs, they can become more sensitive to the world of music around us. They can also learn the purpose of each musical selection and be introduced to general terms for classifying song types.

47. MUSIC IS EVERYWHERE

Materials:
Materials for drawing.

Directions:
Have children examine when and where they hear music during the course of the day: grocery stores, the dentist's office, ball games, television, movie sound tracks, concerts, religious services, and so on.

Discuss what the music is being used for in each situation. Try to help children determine if the music influences how one thinks, feels, or acts. Ask them: "How does this music make you feel?" or "What are the words telling you to do?" See if you can think of a purpose for each musical selection heard.

Next, have children draw pictures of the various places where music may be heard. If doing this activity at school, display these pictures on a bulletin board. If doing this project at home, make the pictures into a book. This will lay the foundation for Activity 48.

48. *USING CHILDREN'S LITERATURE TO DEMONSTRATE THE PURPOSES OF MUSIC*

Materials:
A sampling of picture books based on songs (see titles listed below).

Directions:
Read these books to the children. Then sing the songs upon which the books are based. Ask kids to describe the reason for each song. (Is the song performed when celebrating a holiday? Is it used to help a child fall asleep? Does the song relay information about one's country?) Stress the idea that music acts as a form of communication, as a means of expressing emotions, and as a form of recreation.

During your discussion introduce terms such as *holiday song*, *lullaby*, *work song*, and *patriotic song*. Continue to use these terms in successive activities when discussing song types.

Suggested musical resources:
Picture books based on songs: *Drummer Hoff*; *Follow the Drinking Gourd*; *Frog Went A-Courtin'*; *I Know an Old Lady Who Swallowed a Fly*; *The Little Drummer Boy*; *Mommy, Buy Me a China Doll*; *Old MacDonald Had a Farm*; *Six Little Ducks*; *Skip to My Lou*; *The Star-Spangled Banner*; *Yankee Doodle*.

SOCIAL AND HISTORICAL INFLUENCES

ONCE CHILDREN HAVE BEEN MADE AWARE OF THE SIGNIFICANCE of music in everyone's life, they can easily understand how historical and social events may bring about changes in music. In conjunction with this concept, kids can examine the idea that artists in general use materials that are available to them at the time and place of their endeavors. In the next two activities, children's books will be used to introduce these concepts.

49. WHY WAS THE SONG COMPOSED?

General literature for children:
If You Lived at the Time of the Great San Francisco Earthquake; *If You Sailed on the Mayflower*; *Small Wolf*; or any other books that can be used for studying historical events and/or social situations.

Directions:
Review the idea that music serves many purposes—to accompany acts of recreation, devotion, patriotism, work, and so on. In so doing, review the terms that describe various song types: lullabies, sea chanties, work songs, railroad songs, spirituals, patriotic songs, and the like. Explain to children that social and historical events may result in the composition and performance of certain types of songs.

Next, read at least one of the above books, and discuss the historical event that is the focus of the story. Allow children to suggest the types of songs the characters in the book might sing, play, or compose. Ask them to tell you why. Guide them through this process using the three samples that follow.

Read *If You Sailed on the Mayflower*. Discuss the events that led to this journey. Ask the children what types of songs the early European settlers might have composed, sung, or played—and why. Children may suggest that religious selections were performed to show devotion. They may suggest that songs were sung about leaving one's home in search of a new life.

Read *If You Lived at the Time of the Great San Francisco Earthquake*. Discuss how people of this time had to work together to reshape their lives. Ask children what types of songs might have been sung by the people in the earthquake area. The children may suggest that songs were performed that promoted hope and cooperation.

Read *Small Wolf*. Discuss how Small Wolf's family was displaced by the white man and how his family repeatedly needed to reestablish themselves. Ask children what types of songs his family might have sung as they searched for food, built their home, comforted their children, or spoke to the spirits of nature.

If you have not already done so, this is an excellent time to share picture books that are based on songs and that also have a social or historical theme (see titles listed below).

As a final exercise, sing and listen to songs from early America (see song collections and recordings listed below). Ask children if these songs are sung for the same reasons today as they were when they were composed. Introduce the idea that while some songs may still be sung for the same purposes (lullabies, for example), others, such as work songs or railroad songs once sung to ease workers' sorrows or burdens, may now be sung simply for fun.

Suggested musical resources:
Picture books: *Follow the Drinking Gourd*; *The Star-Spangled Banner*; *Yankee Doodle*. Song collections: *All Night, All Day: A Child's First Book of African-American Spirituals*; *American Folk Songs for Children in Home, School, and Nursery School: A Book for Children, Parents, and Teachers*; *American Indian Music and Musical Instruments*; *Lullabies and Night Songs*. Recordings: *American Folk Songs for Children*; *Pueblo Indians in Story, Song, and Dance*.

50. CREATING A HISTORICAL TIME LINE

Materials:
Recordings of selections from various musical periods (see recording listed below, or obtain additional recordings through your public library system) and magazines containing pictures of artwork, architecture, and clothing from corresponding periods. You may wish to precut these pictures if working with younger children.

Directions:

Play a composition each day from a different musical period. Selections from the Middle Ages, Renaissance, baroque, classical, romantic, and twentieth-century periods should be included in that order.

After studying each musical period, assist children in creating a poster featuring magazine cutouts of corresponding artwork, clothing, architecture, dances, or theatrical productions. Make sure to create a poster to represent each period.

When completed, display these posters where children can enjoy them. Go through the musical selections again, as you reexamine your posters. Discuss how the art forms of a particular period may appear similar. You might wish to use terms to describe these similarities such as *decorative* or *abstract*. Discuss the fact that art forms may reflect a changing society, as well as the materials and technology available within a given time frame or geographical area.

As an additional activity, read books or stories to children about composers (see titles listed below).

Suggested musical resources:

Recording: *Invitation to Music.* Books on composers: *America, I Hear You: A Story About George Gershwin*; *Beethoven*; *Wolferl: The First Six Years in the Life of Wolfgang Amadeus Mozart, 1756–1762*; *Women Music Makers.*

THE MUSICAL CONTRIBUTIONS OF VARIOUS CULTURAL GROUPS

THE FOLLOWING ACTIVITIES WILL INTRODUCE THE FACT THAT PEOPLE of various cultural backgrounds have had a hand in creating a multicultural repertoire of music in America. Through the years, as individuals arrived in this country and made their homes here, they very often continued to take part in the customs unique to their cultural group. In doing so, they shared their customs with others. This means they also shared their songs and musical styles. The music of those who arrived in early America can still be heard along with the music of those who have recently found their homes here. These styles, in combination with the breathtaking array of songs and musical traditions of the Native Americans, create a multitude of options for both the performer and the listener.

In this section, children will first listen as you read picture books that focus on people in various settings. They will learn songs and dances representative of different cultures, and they will discuss the fact that people of different backgrounds have made major contributions in all areas of music. Children can then plan an imaginary trip to an undiscovered place and discuss what the music might be like. They can also create instruments that they feel might be reflective of this culture. Encourage them to discuss how their visit might affect the music of this newly discovered culture.

51. USING LITERATURE TO DEMONSTRATE THE INFLUENCE OF MULTICULTURAL MUSIC

General literature for children:

From Abenaki to Zuni: A Dictionary of Native American Tribes; *Ming Lo Moves the Mountain*; *Miss Rumphius*; *A Picture Book of Jewish Holidays*; *Small Wolf*; *The Snowy Day*; *Strega Nona's Magic Lessons*; *Who's in Rabbit's House? A Masai Tale*; *Why Mosquitoes Buzz in People's Ears: A West African Tale*; or any other books that focus on a particular cultural group.

Directions:

Begin by pointing out that there are a wide variety of cultural groups in the world. Next, read one or more of the books listed above, and ask children what types of music they might hear or sing if they were a character in the story.

Children's answers may be as basic as "Songs with drums" or "Songs with bagpipes." If reading a book that takes place in the United States (such as *The Snowy Day*), they may simply answer with "The same songs we hear." These initial responses are fine. Next, ask the children what would happen if the characters in the book suddenly traveled to another part of the world.

If using *Ming Lo Moves the Mountain*, for example, ask the children what type of songs Ming Lo might bring to America. What types of songs would he sing once he arrived there? Would he perhaps learn Western opera or gospel songs? Would he teach the songs of his country to others? If the little boy in *The Snowy Day* traveled to Asia, would he take with him various styles of music such as popular songs, folk songs, and Afro-American spirituals?

Sing a musical selection or listen to a selection that is representative of the characters in the book or of a specific culture (see titles listed below). Make it a point to mention that our country has a rich collection of music as a result of the numerous groups that have made their homes here.

A wonderful follow-up is to read the book *All of You Was Singing* (see the Annotated Bibliography of Music Literature for Children), which relates the Aztec legend of how music arrived on the earth. Discuss the fact that people of different cultures have different legends about how music came to be.

Suggested musical resources:
Song collections: *All Night, All Day: A Child's First Book of African-American Spirituals*; *American Folk Songs for Children in Home, School, and Nursery School: A Book for Children, Parents, and Teachers*; *American Indian Music and Musical Instruments*; *Lullabies and Night Songs*. Recordings: *American Folk Songs for Children*; *Follow the Sunset: A Beginning Geography Record with Nine Songs from Around the World*; *Lullabies from 'Round the World*; *Pueblo Indians in Story, Song, and Dance*; *Sing Children Sing: Songs of Mexico*; *Sing Children Sing: Songs of the United States of America*.

52. *LEARNING FOLK DANCES*

Materials:

A recording of folk dances from various countries (numerous recordings with directions on dance steps should be available through your public library system).

Directions:

Teach folk dances from a sampling of countries. People in your community can often be wonderful resources when it comes to activities such as these. Try to include dances from a variety of countries both Western and non-Western. Make sure to mention that dances from other parts of the world have influenced the dance styles found in America.

If you are working with your child at home, you may try locating an ethnic dance class in your area and having your child take part in this wonderful experience.

53. *LEARNING THAT MUSICIANS COME FROM DIFFERENT BACKGROUNDS*

Materials:

The two books discussed below.

Directions:

Explain that musicians, composers, conductors, and the like are present in all cultures. Read the books *Ben's Trumpet* (which features characters who are jazz musicians in the United States) and *Pages of Music* (which mentions the shepherd musicians on an island called Sardinia), and point out the differences in racial and cultural backgrounds. Reinforce the idea that people of various cultures and races have made significant contributions to American music.

Suggested musical resources:

Books: *Ben's Trumpet*; *Pages of Music*.

54. EXPLORING MUSIC CREATED FOR AN IMAGINARY PLACE

General literature for children:
The Little Prince.

Materials:
Items for creating handmade instruments.

Directions:
Read the book *The Little Prince*. Plan an imaginary trip to a faraway place. The children may enjoy pretending they are traveling to a mythical planet. Ask the children to describe the clothing, houses, buildings, methods of transportation, and, of course, the music. Discuss the types of instruments played and the style of singing that might be heard.

Next, provide a time for children to create musical instruments that might be found there. Encourage them to be as inventive as possible. Use materials such as paper towel rolls or bits of garden hose (for talking or singing into). Point out the fact that people all over the world and throughout time have created instruments with materials that are available to them.

Finally, ask children what they would tell the inhabitants about American music. Ask the children to imagine how their visit will change the cultural group they have discovered. Discuss what impact it might have on the music of that culture. What effect will their travels have on American music?

CHAPTER EIGHT

Activities for Furthering Musical Appreciation

I N THE PRECEDING ACTIVITIES, MUSICAL EXPERIENCES WERE IN-
troduced using children's literature as a means of discovery.
By now, you may notice that children have begun to display an
obvious appreciation for music. But what exactly is musical
appreciation? Does this mean just listening to opera or learning about jazz?

For our purposes, we will consider musical appreciation to
be a child's display of interest and self-motivation when it
comes to *participating* in musical activities. As we review concepts learned thus far and practice skills that are in the process of being developed, this final activity chapter will also allow the children to demonstrate their acquired appreciation
for music as they are provided with opportunities for listening, performing, and composing.

• *Listening*
Children can learn to listen to music of a variety of styles,
periods, and cultures and decide for themselves which examples they each personally prefer. In doing so, they learn that
voices, instruments, and musical elements may be combined
in a variety of ways, producing numerous forms of music that
are available to the listener.

• *Performing*
Children should be given opportunities to participate in a
planned performance. They enjoy choosing the repertoire for
a performance and deciding how they wish to participate

(sing, dance, etc.). In so doing, they can continue to practice musical skills and develop an understanding that music has many purposes, one of which is to heighten various celebrations.

• *Composing*

Children have fun composing songs and choosing the desired subjects for their compositions (a family member, a news-related item, etc.). In the process, children learn that music may be used to express thoughts and emotions and may reflect social or historical events. Music, like their favorite books, can be used to tell a story!

LISTENING OPTIONS

AT THIS POINT, CHILDREN WILL MOST LIKELY BE SHOWING PREFerences for specific styles of music. A child may enjoy listening to marches or lullabies, symphonies or operas. He or she may show a liking for music from the baroque period or from the continent of Asia.

In this section, children's books will be used as a springboard for discussing personal preferences. After sharing favorite books brought from home, children are encouraged to bring in favorite recordings and to discuss the characteristics (use of voices, instruments, and musical elements) that make the selections appealing to them. Children then take part in a "listening center" where they further demonstrate their preferences for music and continue to examine why they possess such preferences.

55. *USING FAVORITE BOOKS AS A SPRINGBOARD FOR DISCUSSING PERSONAL PREFERENCES*

General literature for children:

Favorite books selected by children.

Directions:

Ask each child to select a favorite book. Ask them to discuss why these are favorites. Some typical responses might include: "I like the colors of the pictures." "I love fairy tales." "Rhyming books are fun." Encourage the development and appreciation of individual tastes. (If doing this activity at home, ask your kids to choose books they would like to hear at bedtime, storytime, etc. Discuss why they like the stories.)

On another occasion, point out that just as people have favorite books, they also have favorite recordings. Encourage each child to select a favorite recording, and listen to them together. Ask a child to explain what it is that makes that recording a favorite. If you are a parent, allow your child to select recordings from your local library. After listening to them, ask children if they enjoyed the selections and to give their reasons. Encourage answers that have to do with specific characteristics of the music, such as "I like the sound of the sitar," or "I like the rhythm."

56. CREATING A LISTENING CENTER

Materials:

Star-shaped stickers and a selection of recordings representing various styles, cultures, and periods. Try to select at least five recordings from various parts of the world (Africa, India, etc.), five from various periods of Western music (baroque, classical, etc.), and five from today's popular musical genres (Western, rock, etc.).

Directions:

Create a comfortable listening center, complete with recordings and a machine that children can easily operate. A child can now demonstrate preferences by rating the recordings with star-shaped stickers. After hearing each recording, young listeners might give it one star if they think they would like to hear it again. If they think they'd like to hear it twice more, a two-star rating is in order. An all-time favorite would receive three stars or more.

If doing this activity at home, a child can place the stickers directly on the album or cassette cover. If doing this activity with a class, each child should receive his or her own list of the recordings and place the stars directly on this list. When all the children have listened to the selections and completed their rating sheets, you may wish to graph the results to determine which recordings or musical styles were overall favorites.

Encourage children to discuss why certain recordings are consistent favorites, and allow the children to listen again to the music that received the highest ratings. Excellent gifts for birthdays and holidays would be additional recordings to add to their listening center.

Variation:

Why not expand this activity and create a personal reading corner as well? Have children rate their favorite books and examine which were favorites by graphing the results.

PERFORMANCE OPTIONS

IN THE FOLLOWING ACTIVITIES, CHILDREN SELECT THE REPERtoire for an upcoming performance and then decide how they wish to perform this repertoire. They begin by listening to books connected with a particular holiday. Some of these books are based on songs, which may be learned and performed as part of this project. Next, youngsters listen to books that focus on characters performing. This activity provides them with ideas for the way in which they would like to participate in their own performance (sing, dance, or play an instrument).

57. USING CHILDREN'S BOOKS AS AN AID IN SELECTING REPERTOIRE

General literature for children:

Chinese New Year; A Friend Is Someone Who Likes You: Silver Anniversary Edition; If You Sailed on the Mayflower; It's Halloween; Leo the Late Bloomer; A Picture Book of Jewish

Holidays; *The Polar Express*; *The Tale of Peter Rabbit*; *The Velveteen Rabbit*; *Where the Wild Things Are: 25th Anniversary Edition*; or any other books that may be used in conjunction with holiday studies.

Directions:

Begin by reading books to children in preparation for an upcoming holiday event. *If You Sailed on the Mayflower* could be read for Thanksgiving; *The Polar Express* or *The Velveteen Rabbit* could be shared for Christmas; *The Tale of Peter Rabbit* is fun at Easter; *Chinese New Year* might be used to explain the customs of this holiday; *Where the Wild Things Are: 25th Anniversary Edition* and *It's Halloween* are fun at Halloween. *A Picture Book of Jewish Holidays* can be used throughout the year. *A Friend Is Someone Who Likes You: Silver Anniversary Edition* is touching on St. Valentine's Day. On birthdays, it's occasionally necessary to discuss how people mature at different rates. *Leo the Late Bloomer* is a perfect introduction to such a discussion.

Ask children what songs or musical selections are representative of the same holiday or event. Kids always enjoy listing their favorite Halloween songs, Thanksgiving songs, Christmas songs, Easter songs, patriotic songs, Hanukkah songs, and so on.

Next, read books that have musical counterparts and that can be used in conjunction with holiday studies (see below for examples of books based on musical selections). If preparing for Christmas, read the book *The Nutcracker*, and then listen to a recording of *The Nutcracker Suite* (obtain a copy through your public library system). Discuss why it would be important to include music in an upcoming performance or event. Remind children that music has many purposes within a culture and one such purpose is to heighten cultural and religious celebrations. With your guidance, allow your young musicians to select the repertoire for an upcoming event.

Suggested musical resources:

Books: *Hilary Knight's The Twelve Days of Christmas*; *The Little Drummer Boy*; *The Nutcracker*; *The Star-Spangled Banner*; *Yankee Doodle*.

58. *HOW DO YOU WISH TO PARTICIPATE?*

General literature for children:
Any books that mention or illustrate characters acting as instrumentalists, singers, conductors, or the like (see titles listed below).

Directions:
Read aloud several books that illustrate the characters singing, playing instruments, dancing, or partaking in music-related activities. Ask children how they would like to participate in their upcoming performance. Would they like to sing, play instruments, or create a dance based on a holiday song? Perhaps some would like to conduct or compose new lyrics to traditional tunes.

Assist children in planning a program around their choices and around the repertoire they selected in Activity 57. Be creative in your planning by including dances learned in other activities or featuring artwork the children have created. Perhaps you would like to plan an entire performance around one of the stories mentioned in Activity 57.

Suggested musical resources:
Books: *Ben's Trumpet*; *The Bremen-Town Musicians*; *Geraldine, the Music Mouse*; *The Little Drummer Boy*; *Mama Don't Allow: Starring Miles and the Swamp Band*; *Music, Music for Everyone*; *Pages of Music*; *The Philharmonic Gets Dressed*; *The Trumpet of the Swan*.

COMPOSING OPTIONS

BY NOW, CHILDREN HAVE LEARNED THAT MUSIC, AS WELL AS other art forms, can be used to communicate feelings, values, and information. In the next activity, they combine composing with the folk art of quilting (which also serves as a means of portraying thoughts and emotions). They choose the topic of their song, compose their selection, and then transfer it to the fabric that will be used for the quilt.

59. MAKING A MUSICAL QUILT

General literature for children:
The Quilt Story.

Materials:
Fabric for making a lap quilt or wall hanging (forty-nine squares of material cut to measure six inches by six inches, batting to measure thirty-five inches by thirty-five inches, one large piece of material measuring thirty-seven inches by thirty-seven inches), thread, yarn, and fabric markers. When selecting material, keep in mind that children will be writing on the fabric. You may, therefore, wish to select solid colors for the squares that will contain writing.

Directions:
Begin by reading *The Quilt Story*. Discuss how quilts may be used to portray feelings or events. Tell children that they will be composing a song and placing it on a quilt. Allow children to select the topic for their composition. They may decide to write about a relative or a news-related item. If working with a group of children, each child may contribute one line of the song. When completed, select a traditional folk tune to accompany the lyrics the children have created. Sing the song as a group.

On another occasion, have each child write his or her original lyrics on a fabric square, using a permanent fabric marker. Young children can dictate their lines to an adult. Lay out the squares so the children may see how it will look. Adult assistance will be required when stitching the quilt together, but this activity in itself may inspire eager volunteers. Sewing and singing go together.

Using a half-inch seam, sew the blocks together with seven squares in each row. Now stitch all rows together. This will be the front of your quilt. When the front is complete, pin it to the batting with the right side facing out and then baste together using a three-eighths-inch seam.

Next, turn under half an inch on all four sides of your large piece of material and press. With wrong sides together, pin the front with batting attached and back together, making sure the front is centered. Then bring the extended edges of the back over the front. Pin in place and top stitch.

If you wish, you may run yarn from the front to the back and then again to the front at each corner where squares meet, and tie into bows.

CHAPTER NINE

A Child's Musical Instruction: Further Steps

N OW THAT YOU HAVE EXPERIENCED THE JOY OF MAKING MUSIC with your child or an entire class, you may be contemplating your next steps. If you are a classroom teacher, you are undoubtedly already thinking of new activities that you would like to try with your current class or next group of students. You may also be excited about sharing your ideas with other teachers and relaying information to your students' parents on the importance and fun of music making. This chapter will provide you with tips on locating additional materials, budgeting time for music during the school day, and getting others (teachers and parents) enthused about music instruction in the classroom and at home.

If you are a parent and are interested in pursuing the idea of combining music with literature or perhaps with other areas of learning, this chapter will give you suggestions for continuing in this direction. If you are interested in involving your child in outside music classes or lessons, you will find guidelines here for finding the best schools and instructors and for interviewing and observing music teachers. In addition, you will learn how to be supportive of your child's private lessons as well as his or her school music program.

FOR TEACHERS

FINDING AND USING ADDITIONAL MATERIALS

To assure your continued success in the teaching of music—whether you are a teacher or a parent—you should keep the following points in mind. Materials for teaching the basics of music need not be expensive, nor do they need to be difficult to locate. You can instead continue to create wonderfully enriching experiences for children using picture books, song collections, and recordings from your own public or school library. You may also use items that children choose or make themselves.

Finding the time to teach music should now be easier than previously imagined. Why not now try combining music with other subjects or even with the daily classroom routine?

If you are a teacher, let parents know about your musical goals. Once parents are informed, and begin to see positive outcomes, many will be happy to donate rhythm instruments, project materials, and the like. Some parents will be willing to volunteer their time to assist the children in the process of learning songs and dances for special units or performances. Other teachers often only need to hear positive comments from parents and children before getting involved themselves. Here are some tips for proceeding further.

• When looking for additional resources that pertain to music (or any other subject for that matter), consult the numerous reference books on the market that list children's materials. Two excellent books that I've come to rely on as a teacher and as a parent are *Best Books for Children: Preschool Through Grade Six* and *The Elementary School Library Collection: A Guide to Books and Other Media*. A librarian can help you find other references.

• *The Phonolog Reports* are an exceptional way of finding the most current recordings available. Many audio stores receive such listings and make them available for customers to browse through.

● If you are a classroom teacher, let the school music teacher know about your intention to include more musical activities in your lesson plans. He or she may be able to suggest additional resources for you to try.

● Shops that offer musical instruments for sale or rent often have books that are helpful.

● Try to include at least one musical activity in daily teaching plans. Once this becomes part of a classroom routine, children will miss its absence.

● Teachers can integrate musical activities not only with other subject areas but with everyday classroom happenings. Echo clapping, for example, can act as a signal to children that it is time to stop and listen. Recordings can be played during silent reading time. But don't fall into the trap of using music only as a supplement. Make sure you continue to discuss musical elements and continue to involve children in the development of musical skills.

SEVEN WAYS TEACHERS CAN GET OTHERS INVOLVED IN MUSICAL ACTIVITIES

1.   Inform parents about upcoming musical units and/or school or community performances on notes sent home or on weekly assignment sheets.

2.   Pass on information to parents about books on the topic of music.

3.   Have children put together a display featuring original compositions or handmade instruments. This is a wonderful way of getting others interested.

4.   Have children assist students in another class with the making of a musical instrument or other music-related project.

5.   Allow children to gain the most from their school music teacher. Be sure they are ready when it's time for the music teacher to take over. Understand that it is necessary at times for children to be pulled out of class for band rehearsals, chorus practice, and the like. Stress the importance of these activities when others complain about pull-out schedules or the time that music takes away from other subjects.

6.   Attend workshops on music, and share information with your teaching peers and parents.

7.   Encourage adults who lack self-confidence with musical activities to relax and shed their inhibitions. Children are not concerned with how well their teachers or parents sing or play. But they do notice if a teacher or parent never partakes in musical activities.

FOR PARENTS

AS A PARENT WHO HAS ALREADY INTRODUCED YOUR CHILD TO THE basics of a well-rounded musical curriculum, you are in a better position than most to predict what musical activity your youngster may enjoy next. Perhaps you and your child have been quite happy working on projects at home and wish to continue in this manner.

Or maybe your child is excited about joining a group class, which can be a highly motivating and socially rewarding experience. A basic music class, one which reviews the musical elements that you have introduced and which involves the child in skill-based activities, may be the perfect next step at this time. Because of your diligent work at home, your child may be able to skip a beginners class and enter at a more advanced level. If your child has been exhibiting an interest in a specific instrument or in singing, this may be the time to enroll him or her in a group instrumental class, a chorus, or possibly in private instruction. No matter which avenue you decide to pursue, you will find the following suggestions can improve a child's chances of success.

CONTINUING AT HOME

If, for the time being, you have decided to continue music education at home with your child, you may want to take a few moments and set some long-range goals for both you and your youngster.

• Part of your plans should be to review the concepts that have been introduced thus far and to continue to develop musical skills. You might do this by going through the activities in this book a second or third time—or even more often. Because numerous resources are listed here, you will be able to use the activities again and again, each time creating a new experience for your child.

• Once you feel that you would like to locate some additional children's resources, ask your local librarian for suggested books that would be of interest to your particular child.

• Make it a personal commitment to take your child to at least one musical performance a month. It is not necessary for these to be costly or even all of professional quality. Children should be exposed to musical performances that involve other children, as well as college and community groups. Make it a yearly treat (at least) to take the entire family to see a full-blown professional production.

• Teach your child good audience etiquette. Talk about the performance before or after, *not during*. Talking during a performance is extremely annoying to all those around you, including the performers.

• Seek out ways for your child to share his or her musical interest with your community. At a local county fair, for example, children are encouraged to enter original musical compositions for exhibition and judging. There may be musical organizations within your area that promote other musical events for children.

• Show your child that you "practice what you preach." Join a local community chorus or band. If you truly lack the confidence to do so, at least volunteer to assist the group with rehearsals, fund-raisers, or performances.

SEEKING OUTSIDE INSTRUCTION

When the time has come to involve your child in lessons outside the home, the first step will be for you to investigate the various offerings in your area. There are a number of ways to obtain the names of reputable instructors or music schools.

- Start by checking your local phone listings. Private music teachers and music schools that are in the regular business of providing instruction are usually listed.
- Ask your local college music department for a list of teachers in the area.
- Check with local music stores to obtain additional names of music instructors in your area that specialize in working with children.
- See if there is a local branch of the Music Teachers' Association or any other music organization in your area that may be able to give you suggestions.
- Ask musicians that you know personally to recommend teachers or classes that might be appropriate for your child.

Twelve Questions to Ask a Music Teacher

Once you are equipped with a list of possible instructors or classes, your next step is to interview several individuals. This initial interview may be done efficiently over the phone. Be prepared to jot down the answers as you ask each candidate a variety of questions.

1.   If searching for a basic music class, or instrumental or choral group, begin by asking the teacher if a course description can be sent to you (see sample course descriptions that follow these questions). If a course description is not available, have the teacher explain to you in detail what will be covered in the class.

2.   Ask for a brief explanation of how overall goals are broken down in each class meeting or practice session. The teacher should make it clear to you that although various items may be introduced, children naturally progress at different rates and the mastery of these items will vary from child to child.

3.   Let the teacher know what your child has already accomplished at home, and ask if the class you are investigating will match your child's present abilities.

4.   If your child is shy or overly excitable, ask how these traits are handled by the instructor.

5.   Ask the teacher about his or her musical background and teaching background. (Experience in both areas is essential.)

6.   Ask the teacher what ages he or she prefers to teach and why.

7.   Ask the teacher to describe the components of a comprehensive music class. You, of course, are now aware of what these components should be.

8.   Ask the teacher for references from parents. (If supplied, ask the parents to describe their children's current attitudes toward music.)

9.   Make sure you understand all policies and procedures concerning payments, make-up lessons, and so forth (these items will vary from teacher to teacher). A teacher working out of his or her home, for example, may not charge as much as a teacher working out of a store because of decreased overhead. If this teacher is a concert pianist or has an extensive background in teaching, however, the fees charged may be deservedly higher than those of other teachers you interview.

10.   Ask if the teacher has recently taken part in workshops or in-service training, or is a member of a performing group and/or professional music association. Try to find a teacher who demonstrates an obvious affection for music as well as an interest in self-improvement.

11.   Ask about performance opportunities and requirements. It is my personal opinion that children should be given the opportunity to perform but should never be forced to do so.

12.   Ask if the instructor subscribes to a certain method of teaching. Some teachers are zealots about a specific musical method, whereas others use a more eclectic approach to teaching. Regardless of the method(s) used, the teacher should be able to clearly explain the reasons for adopting this approach. The teacher should also be able to inform you of the method's strengths and weaknesses, and to speak knowledgeably about other methods of instruction.

Here are brief descriptions of widely used methods that may be mentioned:

Dalcroze Eurhythmics. Émile Jaques-Dalcroze (1865–1950), a Swiss teacher and composer, developed a method that focuses on creative movement to introduce musical concepts.

Kodály Method. The Hungarian Zoltán Kodály (1882–1967) was a music educator, composer, and collector of folk music. His method concentrates on the voice as the primary instrument. Concepts are introduced sequentially through songs that are native to the child's land. Hand signals are employed to assist with pitch matching and interval study, and rhythmic syllables are used to teach the child to read and write rhythmic patterns.

Orff-Schulwerk. This method was developed by Carl Orff (1895–1982), a German composer and educator. It makes frequent use of instruments created by Orff in order to introduce musical elements and to enhance musical skills. Children are encouraged to create songs and respond to music through movement.

Suzuki. Developed by the Japanese educator Shin'ichi Suzuki (1898–), this method was originally used to instruct children on the violin. It is now employed in the teaching of other instruments as well. Through rote learning, repetition, imitation, and listening to recordings, children learn to play selections immediately; note reading is introduced at a later date through songs the children have already learned to play. Parents are encouraged to assist in the child's learning process.

Sample Class Descriptions

I wrote the following descriptions for three music classes I teach at a local preschool (the Rainbow Bridge Montessori School): a beginning musicianship class, a recorder class, and a keyboard class.

The Beginning Musicianship Class is a semester-long course and is open to students between the ages of three and five. An instructional approach is used which blends the methodologies of Kodály, Orff, and Dalcroze into a musical curriculum that is both complete and enjoyable. The children are introduced to basic musical elements (beat, rhythm, melody, form, dynamics, tempo, etc.) in a sequential and age-appropriate manner through singing, music reading and writing, movement, music appreciation, and instrumental activities. An emphasis is placed on American songs and singing games and musical instruments and styles of the Western culture.

The Recorder Class is open to students who have completed the Beginning Musicianship Class. All aspects of the Beginning Class are reviewed first. Skills are then strengthened as the students learn to play and create simple melodies on the recorder. An emphasis is placed on the study of songs, dances, and instruments of various cultures.

The Keyboard Class is open to kindergartners who have had two full semesters of music or by special permission of the instructor. Instruction combines singing, reading, writing, composing, and keyboard skills into a balanced and fun curriculum. The children continue to strengthen the skills developed in previous classes, with an emphasis being placed on reading music in preparation for private study on any musical instrument.

Observing a Music Teacher in Action

The next step in your search should be fun for both you and your child. It is always exciting to observe the many ways music may be taught. In order to select what is most appropriate for your child, it is essential that you observe a variety of settings before making a final decision. When observing, you may want to keep a mental checklist of what occurs. Here's what you'll be looking for:

- The teacher should recognize that each child is different and should treat each child as a special, unique individual.
- The teacher should be positive when correcting the child.
- The teacher should possess a sense of humor.

When observing a general music class:

- The teacher's directions should always be clear, and the children should be encouraged to ask questions.
- The room should be large enough to comfortably accommodate the number of children enrolled (as well as their parents).
- The teacher should vary the activities and songs. A mixture of singing, movement, and other activities will keep the kids interested.
- The teacher should make it a habit to explain and/or practice a concept in a variety of ways (if discussing a rhythmic pattern, for example, the children should sing the pattern, clap the pattern, play the pattern, etc.).
- When visual aids are used, all children should be able to see the materials.
- There should be enough rhythm instruments, barred instruments, and other materials for each child in the class.

When observing a keyboard class or other instrumental class:

- All the children should have instruments.
- There should be enough music stands for everyone to read comfortably.
- Instruction should be given on breathing, intonation, proper hand placement, tuning, and the like.
- The materials should be appropriate for all the children in the class.
- The teacher should instruct the children on how to properly care for their instruments and give them enough time to do so.

When observing a vocal lesson or practice:

- The teacher should take the time to warm up the students' voices.
- The repertoire should be varied, with the possible inclusion of songs in different languages.

- The teacher should appear knowledgeable about vocal techniques, breathing, and intonation.
- The teacher should use some type of methodology to promote music reading and sight-singing.

When observing a private lesson:

- The teacher should tailor instruction to fit the child's current needs.
- The teacher should provide the child with a clear, written assignment.

ONCE YOUR CHILD HAS STARTED LESSONS . . .

At this point, it is important to be aware of what happens each week both in and out of music lessons. It is essential that you have an open and frank relationship with your child's teacher. To make sure your child is getting the most out of lesson time, you should know what to expect from the teacher:

- The teacher should give your child an appropriate amount of material each week. Occasionally, your child may appear to have too much or too little work. If this is always the case, mention it to the instructor.
- Clear, written assignments should be given by the instructor each week. If the teacher is not in the practice of doing this, request that it be done.
- If a small child is involved, the teacher should verbally discuss your child's assignment with you after each lesson. Initiate the conversation if the teacher doesn't. Assume that this conversation will take place at the end of your own child's lesson time, not during the beginning of the next child's lesson.
- The teacher should periodically make it a habit to inform you of your child's progress.
- The teacher should keep the environment pleasant, comfortable, and free from as many distractions as possible (some things may be impossible to control, depending on the setting).

- The teacher should offer suggestions for making practicing a pleasant routine.
- The teacher should be receptive to any concerns you may have.
- The teacher should encourage you to observe at various times during the year.

Eight Suggestions to Help Your Child Stay on Task

Now that your child is taking group or private lessons, how can you increase the odds that he or she will continue with this instruction? I believe that the key to success is in simply helping your child become and stay organized. Here are eight ideas for doing just that:

1.   Help your child prepare for the start of music lessons just as you would at the beginning of a new school year. Make sure the child has all the required materials, including a book bag or backpack for storing music items (so that materials do not get misplaced). Do a periodic check to see which items need to be replaced.

2.   Make sure your child takes all music books to each lesson. Inconsistency in this regard often influences how the child views these lessons in general. When the result is inconsistent practice, the child may not make any progress. Unable to understand why, he or she may want to quit out of frustration.

3.   After each lesson, ask your child to explain what was covered. Read through your child's written lesson together, and encourage your child to practice key items immediately after the lesson, thus reinforcing his or her learning.

4.   Children may need a gentle reminder about practicing at home. Set up an incentive program to encourage self-motivation. The parent of one of my students places stickers on a chart each time the child practices independently. After a designated number of stickers is earned, the child gets to select a new book from the bookstore.

5.   Encourage your child to practice at a regular time *every* day. Choose a time that does not conflict with other household activities and when the child is not likely to

be interrupted. Since our piano is in use the entire after-
noon by my private students, both my children are required
to practice their lessons in the morning before school or
other activities. But I often hear my children practicing a
second time in the evening, playing songs solely for their own
enjoyment.

6.   Help your children when they ask for it or when
it's suggested by the teacher. Most beginning method books
are self-explanatory. A parent with very little background in
music can help the child overcome a stumbling block that
might otherwise have led to a wasted week.

7.   Once you have gone to all the trouble of selecting
a teacher, trust the teacher and allow the child to do his
very best. Some children do better when a parent is
present during the lesson. But others find the presence of
a parent to be a distraction. In the initial stages of lessons,
you may want to try attending some sessions and not others,
and then ask the teacher in which situation the child did
better.

8.   Show your support for your child's musical endeavors by attending all performances. I also make it a habit
to give my children a small token (such as a flower) after each
performance. Such a token can heighten a child's sense of
accomplishment—and serve as a source of comfort in case the
performance did not go well.

TEN WAYS YOU CAN SUPPORT YOUR CHILD'S SCHOOL MUSIC PROGRAM

If your child attends a school where a music program is in
existence, you are truly fortunate. As more and more schools
face shrinking budgets, school music programs are unfortunately feeling the effects. It is of utmost importance that you,
as a parent, voice your opinions about the necessity of music
in the curriculum. This can be accomplished in a variety of
positive ways.

1.   Attend any site council meetings or school board
meetings where changes to the school music program may be
discussed.

2.   After a performance, write a personal note to the teacher in charge, thanking him or her for the time and energy devoted to the children.

3.   Write a note to the principal or school board about your happiness with a music teacher or with a particular musical performance.

4.   Let the music teacher know that you are supportive of a comprehensive music program—a program that includes all aspects of music education and covers all genres of music.

5.   On school surveys, voice your opinions on changes that need to occur to improve the school music program or offerings.

6.   If music seems to be lacking from the curriculum, bring this issue to the attention of your child's classroom teacher or school principal.

7.   Donate to the school any extra instruments or musical materials that may be in your house. But make sure you leave some items at home for your child to enjoy.

8.   Send in interesting musical items with your child so they can be shared in class.

9.   Send in to your child's classroom teacher or music teacher information about interesting books or articles you've read.

10.   Be an active partner by assisting in whatever way possible. Volunteer to help out in your child's classroom music program, band class, or choir. Even if you can't read music, there are many ways to help. Perhaps you could catalog sheet music, organize a collection of music books and tapes, help record the band, or even bring snacks to the singers.

This last tip is perhaps the most crucial. For children to participate in, create, and appreciate music, they must see the adults around them doing the same. Music is fun for all ages. Above all, classroom teachers, music teachers, and parents should work together toward the common goal of creating accessible and enjoyable musical experiences for children.

PART 2

Annotated Bibliography of General Literature for Children

This bibliography comprises those books that are listed in Part I under "general literature for children." The books are also cited in the subject guide.

BLACK IS BROWN IS TAN by Arnold Adoff. Illustrated by Emily A. McCully. New York: HarperCollins, 1973. 32 pages. Colored illustrations. Grades: Preschool–3. *This picture book covers a topic that is rarely discussed with children: the interracial family. The members of this family are close and care for one another. An imaginative rhyme is used to tell their story.*

BROWN BEAR, BROWN BEAR, WHAT DO YOU SEE? by Bill Martin, Jr. Illustrated by Eric Carle. New York: Henry Holt, 1983. 24 pages. Colored illustrations. Grades: Preschool–1. *This wonderful book uses a repetitive rhyme, an assortment of animals, and audience participation to introduce colors.*

CAPS FOR SALE: A TALE OF A PEDDLER, SOME MONKEYS, AND THEIR MONKEY BUSINESS by Esphyr Slobodkina. New York: HarperCollins, 1947. 43 pages. Colored illustrations. Grades: Preschool–2. *When a peddler decides to take a nap, several monkeys snatch his caps. The ensuing shenanigans make for a humorous story.*

CHARLIE AND THE CHOCOLATE FACTORY by Roald Dahl. Illustrated by Joseph Schindelman. New York: Knopf, 1991 (originally published in 1964). 162 pages. Illustrated. Grades: 1–6. *Mr. Willy Wonka owns a fabulous chocolate factory, and five children have won the opportunity to tour it. One of the youngsters is a sensitive, kind boy named Charlie. As the other four children fail to follow Mr. Wonka's directions, they are each taught an astonishing lesson. Charlie, however, receives a surprise beyond belief at the end of the humorous tour.*

CHARLOTTE'S WEB by E. B. White. Illustrated by Garth Williams. New York: HarperCollins, 1952. 184 pages. Illustrated. Grades: 2–6. *The unforgettable story of Charlotte, an amazing spider who saves a pig named Wilbur from a terrible fate. Other characters include a little girl named Fern and a rat named Templeton. (A Newbery Medal Honor Book, 1953; George G. Stone Center for Children's Books Recognition of Merit Award, 1970; Michigan Young Readers' Award, 1980)*

CHICKENS AREN'T THE ONLY ONES by Ruth Heller. New York: Putnam, Grosset & Dunlap, 1981. 40 pages. Colored illustrations. Grades: Preschool–2. *Creatures that are oviparous are described in rhyme in this beautifully illustrated work. (An honorable mention for the New York Academy of Sciences Children's Science Book Award)*

CHINESE NEW YEAR by Tricia Brown. Photographs by Fran Ortiz. New York: Henry Holt, 1987. 48 pages. Colored photographs. Grades: K–6. *This informative book discusses the traditional customs connected with the Chinese New Year.*

DANNY, THE CHAMPION OF THE WORLD by Roald Dahl. Illustrated by Jill Bennett. New York: Knopf, 1975. 198 pages. Illustrated. Grades: 3–6. *Danny and his father take part in an adventure that is humorous and exciting. A very special look at a father-son relationship.*

A FRIEND IS SOMEONE WHO LIKES YOU: SILVER ANNIVERSARY EDITION by Joan Walsh Anglund. San Diego, Calif.: Harcourt Brace Jovanovich, 1983 (originally published in 1958). 32 pages. Colored illustrations. Grades: Preschool–3. *This charming tale reminds us that a friend can always be found. The illustrations are heartwarming. (One of the* New York Times's *Best Illustrated Children's Books, 1958)*

FROG AND TOAD ARE FRIENDS by Arnold Lobel. New York: HarperCollins, 1970. 64 pages. Colored illustrations. Grades: K–2. *These five short tales about a frog and a toad are humorous and touching, and exemplify what it means to be a best friend. (A Caldecott Medal Honor Book Finalist, 1971, and a finalist for the National Book Award for Children's Literature, 1971) Other books in the series include:* Frog and Toad Together, Frog and Toad All Year, *and* Days with Frog and Toad.

FROM ABENAKI TO ZUNI: A DICTIONARY OF NATIVE AMERICAN TRIBES by Evelyn Wolfson. Illustrated by William Sauts Bock. New York: Walker, 1988. 215 pages. Illustrated. Grades: 4–adult. *This reference book contains information on sixty-eight Native American tribes. An excellent resource for the classroom teacher or parent.*

GOODNIGHT MOON by Margaret Wise Brown. Illustrated by Clement Hurd. New York: HarperCollins, 1947. 30 pages. Colored illustrations. Grades: Preschool–1. *A wonderful bedtime book starring a sleepy bunny who says goodnight to the moon and various objects in his room. This story in rhyme is also available as a pop-up book entitled* The Goodnight Moon Room: A Pop-Up Book.

A HOUSE IS A HOUSE FOR ME by Mary Ann Hoberman. Illustrated by Betty Fraser. New York: Viking Children's Books, 1978. 48 pages. Colored illustrations. Grades: K–3. *The homes of a variety of objects and animals are creatively introduced in this picture book. The text is set in rhyme, and the pictures are delightful. (American Book Award for Best Picture Book, Paperback, 1983)*

IF YOU LIVED AT THE TIME OF THE GREAT SAN FRANCISCO EARTHQUAKE by Ellen Levine. Illustrated by Richard Williams. New York: Scholastic, 1987. 64 pages. Illustrated. Grades: 2–5. *The 1906 earthquake, and the events that followed it, are discussed in question-and-answer format.*

IF YOU SAILED ON THE MAYFLOWER by Ann McGovern. Illustrated by J. B. Handelsman. New York: Scholastic, 1985. 78 pages. Illustrated. Grades: K–4. *This book discusses the journey of the* Mayflower, *the settlement in the New World, and the observance of the first Thanksgiving. It is written in question-and-answer style. Other books in this Scholastic series are equally informative.*

IT'S HALLOWEEN by Jack Prelutsky. Illustrated by Marylin Hafner. New York: Greenwillow Books, 1977. 56 pages. Colored illustrations. Grades: K–3. *Children are sure to enjoy this collection of thirteen short Halloween poems. Parents and teachers will also find the books* It's Thanksgiving *and* It's Valentine's Day *(both also by Prelutsky) to be wonderful additions to holiday studies.*

JAMES AND THE GIANT PEACH: A CHILDREN'S STORY by Roald Dahl. Illustrated by Nancy Ekholm Burkert. New York: Knopf, 1962. 120 pages. Colored illustrations. Grades: 3–6. *James, who goes to live with his two eccentric aunts following the deaths of both his parents, soon becomes involved in an unbelievable adventure with some lovable giant insects and an incredible giant peach. (Massachusetts Children's Book Awards, Grades 4–6, 1982)*

LEO THE LATE BLOOMER by Robert Kraus. Illustrated by Jose Aruego. New York: HarperCollins, Crowell, 1971. 32 pages. Colored illustrations. Grades: Preschool–2. *Little Leo is a tiger who seems young in his ways. Father tiger is concerned because Leo doesn't seem to be able to do the things that other cubs can do. As Leo grows up, however, changes occur. The perfect story for children who sometimes feel that "growing up" will never happen.*

THE LITTLE PRINCE by Antoine de Saint-Exupery. Translated by Katherine Woods. San Diego, Calif.: Harcourt Brace Jovanovich, 1943. 93 pages. Colored illustrations. Grades: 2–adult. *While searching for wisdom, a little prince encounters numerous adventures. An enchanting book.*

THE LITTLE RED HEN retold by Paul Galdone. Boston: Houghton Mifflin, Clarion Books, 1979 (originally published in 1973). 40 pages. Colored illustrations. Grades: Preschool–1. *None of the Little Red Hen's friends are willing to help her plant, tend the wheat, go to the mill, or bake a cake. Her friends soon learn that cooperation is essential if one hopes to share in the rewards.*

MILLIONS OF CATS by Wanda Gag. New York: Putnam, Coward-McCann, 1977 (originally published in 1928). 32 pages. Illustrated. Grades: Preschool–2. *A peasant and his wife decide that a kitten would cure their loneliness. It is a humorous tale indeed when they encounter "hundreds of cats, thousands of cats, millions and billions and trillions of cats." (A Newbery Medal Honor Book, 1929)*

MING LO MOVES THE MOUNTAIN by Arnold Lobel. New York: Greenwillow Books, 1982. 29 pages. Colored illustrations. Grades: Preschool–2. *Ming Lo and his wife live in China. When Ming Lo's wife encourages her husband to move the mountain under which they live, Ming Lo takes the problem to the local wise man. After issuing advice on several occasions, the wise man finally makes a successful suggestion. Children are sure to enjoy the humorous ending to this tale. (Parents' Choice Award for Best Illustrations in Children's Books, 1982)*

MISS RUMPHIUS by Barbara Cooney. New York: Viking Children's Books, 1982. 32 pages. Colored illustrations. Grades: Preschool–3. *As a little girl, Miss Rumphius dreamed of someday traveling to faraway places. She later fulfilled this dream. She also followed the advice of her grandfather; she did "something to make the world more beautiful." A wonderful look at a special aunt and her interest in flowers. (American Book Award for Best Hardback Picture Book, 1983)*

THE NEW KID ON THE BLOCK by Jack Prelutsky. Illustrated by James Stevenson. New York: Greenwillow Books, 1984. 160 pages. Illustrated. Grades: 1–6. *All kinds of things imaginable, from odd creatures to a four-leaf clover, are mentioned in this collection of contemporary American poetry. Children will find the humor and the creativity of these poems enjoyable. (One of the* School Library Journal's *Best Books, 1984)*

A PICTURE BOOK OF JEWISH HOLIDAYS by David A. Adler. Illustrated by Linda Heller. New York: Holiday House, 1981. 32 pages. Colored illustrations. Grades: K–4. *This book provides information on a variety of Jewish holidays. The illustrations are wonderful accompaniments to the text. An excellent resource for the classroom teacher.*

THE POLAR EXPRESS by Chris Van Allsburg. Boston: Houghton Mifflin, 1985. 32 pages. Colored illustrations. Grades: Preschool–adult. *Children of all ages will enjoy this Christmas story about a little boy who travels on a very special train to meet Santa at the North Pole. Once there, he receives a special gift. The outcome will make a believer out of all of us. This is without a doubt my personal favorite. (Caldecott Medal, 1986)*

THE QUILT STORY by Tony Johnston. Illustrated by Tomie De Paola. New York: Putnam, G. P. Putnam's Sons, 1985. 32 pages. Colored illustrations. Grades: Preschool–3. *Two little girls, generations apart, find comfort in the exact same quilt for the exact same reason. A good supplement to a discussion on moving and a beautiful look at mothers and daughters.*

THE RANDOM HOUSE BOOK OF MOTHER GOOSE: A TREASURY OF 306 TIMELESS NURSERY RHYMES. Illustrated by Arnold Lobel. New York: Random House, Random Juvenial, 1986. 176 pages. Colored illustrations. Grades: Preschool–up. *A wonderfully illustrated collection of Mother Goose rhymes. The book contains an index of first lines.*

SING A SONG OF POPCORN: EVERY CHILD'S BOOK OF POEMS selected by Beatrice Schenk De Regniers, Eva Moore, Mary Michaels White, and Jan Carr. Illustrated by a variety of outstanding children's illustrators. New York: Scholastic, Scholastic Hardcover, 1988. 160 pages. Colored illustrations. Grades: Preschool–adult. *This collection of 128 poems is illustrated by such Caldecott Medal artists as Marcia Brown, Leo and Diane Dillon, Richard Egielski, Trina Schart Hyman, Arnold Lobel, Maurice Sendak, Marc Simont, and Margot Zemach. The poems are by Emily Dickinson, Shel Silverstein, and other notable authors. An excellent introduction to poetry. (One of the* School Library Journal's *Best Books, 1988, and one of the American Library Association's Notable Books for Children, 1988)*

THE SKY IS FULL OF SONG selected by Lee Bennett Hopkins. Illustrated by Dirk Zimmer. New York: HarperCollins, 1983. 46 pages. Colored illustrations. Grades 1–6. *A collection of poems written by a variety of authors, including Eve Merriam, Lilian Moore, Karla Kuskin, and Maurice Sendak. Children of all ages will find pleasure in the thirty-eight seasonal poems in this book. (American Institute of Graphic Arts Book Show, children's book show, 1984)*

SMALL WOLF by Nathaniel Benchley. Illustrated by Joan Sandin. New York: HarperCollins, 1972. 64 pages. Colored illustrations. Grades: K–3. *After discovering the presence of white people on Manhattan Island, Small Wolf, an Indian boy, and his family are unfairly displaced.*

THE SNOWY DAY by Ezra Jack Keats. New York: Viking Children's Books, 1962. 34 pages. Colored illustrations. Grades: Preschool–1. *An enchanting story of a young black child and his adventures on a snowy day in the city. (Caldecott Medal, 1963) Another similar and excellent book by the same author is* Whistle for Willie.

STREGA NONA'S MAGIC LESSONS by Tomie De Paola. San Diego, Calif.: Harcourt Brace Jovanovich, 1982. 32 pages. Colored illustrations. Grades: Preschool–3. *Bambolona goes to see Strega Nona, the wise woman, for advice on how to deal with all the work she must do. Meanwhile, Big Anthony takes on a disguise so that he too may study magic with Strega Nona. This is the sequel to* Strega Nona, *which won numerous awards.*

THE TALE OF PETER RABBIT by Beatrix Potter. New York: Frederick Warne, 1987 (originally published in 1902). 58 pages. Colored illustrations. Grades: Preschool–2. *The touching story of Peter Rabbit and Mr. McGregor's garden will remain a favorite among children forever. The book is also available in a variety of languages, including French and Spanish. This is one of a series of books by Potter.*

TOO MUCH NOISE by Ann McGovern. Illustrated by Simms Taback. Boston: Houghton Mifflin, 1967. 44 pages. Colored illustrations. Grades: K–2. *Peter's house is filled with all kinds of noises. These annoying sounds cause Peter to go to the wise man in his village for advice. Peter finds his house filled with even more noise before the humorous climax of this book.*

THE VELVETEEN RABBIT by Margery Williams. Illustrations by David Jorgensen. New York: Knopf, 1985 (originally published in 1922). 47 pages. Colored illustrations. Grades: Preschool–adult. *The Velveteen Rabbit is a stuffed animal who longs to be made real. His friend, the skin horse, informs him that this can only happen after a young child has loved a toy very much and for a long time. After the young boy who owns the rabbit becomes very ill, the Velveteen Rabbit at last gets his wish.*

THE VERY HUNGRY CATERPILLAR by Eric Carle. New York: Putnam, Philomel, 1981 (originally published in 1969). 26 pages. Colored illustrations. Grades: Preschool–2. *An extremely hungry caterpillar literally eats through the pages of this book as the days of the week are introduced. The change he undergoes in the end will delight the young child.*

WHERE THE WILD THINGS ARE: 25TH ANNIVERSARY EDITION by Maurice Sendak. New York: HarperCollins, 1988 (originally published in 1963). 48 pages. Colored illustrations. Grades: Preschool–3. *What do you do when you're sent to your room? You could sail away to "Where the Wild Things Are." This is the tale of Max and such an adventure. The wild things make him their king, but Max soon wants to return home. Once back in his room, he finds his supper waiting for him. (Caldecott Medal, 1964; one of the* New York Times's *Best Illustrated Children's Books of the year, 1963)*

WHO'S IN RABBIT'S HOUSE? A MASAI TALE by Verna Aardema. Illustrated by Leo and Diane Dillon. New York: Dial, 1977. 32 pages. Colored illustrations. Grades: K–3. *The Long One (a caterpillar) is inside Rabbit's house and refuses to leave. Rabbit's friends offer various suggestions. The illustrations are presented as though the characters are actors performing in a Masai village.*

WHY MOSQUITOES BUZZ IN PEOPLE'S EARS: A WEST AFRICAN TALE by Verna Aardema. Illustrated by Leo and Diane Dillon. New York: Dial, 1975. 32 pages. Colored illustrations. Grades: Preschool–4. *A mosquito tells an untruth, which sets off havoc in the jungle. Eventually peace is restored, and the outcome reveals the meaning of the mosquito's buzz. The color illustrations are brilliant. (Caldecott Medal, 1976)*

Annotated
Bibliography of Music
Literature for Children

This bibliography contains a variety of books that are listed in Part I under "suggested musical resources." Included are picture books based on songs, books with music as a central theme, song collections, and books on such music-related topics as the construction of rhythm instruments and the lives of composers. These books are also included in the Subject Guide.

ALL NIGHT, ALL DAY: A CHILD'S FIRST BOOK OF AFRICAN-AMERICAN SPIRITUALS compiled by Ashley Bryan. New York: Macmillan, Atheneum, 1991. 48 pages. Colored illustrations. Grades K–6. *This beautifully illustrated collection of spirituals includes words, guitar chords, and piano arrangements. (Coretta Scott King Illustrator Honor Book Award, 1992)*

ALL OF YOU WAS SINGING retold by Richard Lewis. Artwork by Ed Young. New York: Macmillan, Atheneum, 1991. 32 pages. Colored illustrations. Grades: K–adult. *This Aztec myth focuses on how music arrived on the earth. The illustrations are lovely.*

AMERICA, I HEAR YOU: A STORY ABOUT GEORGE GERSHWIN by Barbara Mitchell. Illustrated by Jan Hosking Smith. Minneapolis: Carolrhoda Books, 1987. 56 pages. Illustrated. Grades: 3–6. *The life and compositions of this great American composer are discussed in an easy-to-understand book.*

AMERICAN FOLK SONGS FOR CHILDREN IN HOME, SCHOOL, AND NURSERY SCHOOL: A BOOK FOR CHILDREN, PARENTS, AND TEACHERS compiled by Ruth Crawford Seeger. Illustrated by Barbara Cooney. New York: Doubleday, Zephyr, 1980 (originally published in 1948). 192 pages. Illustrated with music. Grades: Preschool–adult. *Included in this wonderful collection are lullabies, spirituals, work songs, and more. Melodies with piano accompaniments and guitar chords are provided. Introductory chapters, a subject index, and song title index are helpful.*

AMERICAN INDIAN MUSIC AND MUSICAL INSTRUMENTS by George S. Fichter. Illustrated by Marie and Nils Ostberg. New York: David McKay, 1978. 115 pages. Illustrated. Grades: 3–adult. *This book provides interesting information on the music and musical instruments of Native Americans. Instructions for making basic instruments are included, although adult assistance is required in many cases. Words to some songs are provided, along with a few melodies. Also included are a map and a listing of tribes, as well as pictorial symbols that may be used when decorating instruments.*

BARN DANCE! by Bill Martin, Jr., and John Archambault. Illustrated by Ted Rand. New York: Henry Holt, 1986. 32 pages. Colored illustrations. Grades: Preschool–3. *In this tale, a little boy tiptoes out to the barn where a whimsical barn dance is taking place.*

BEETHOVEN by Alan Blackwood. Illustrated by Richard Hook. New York: Franklin-Watts, Bookwright Press, 1987. 32 pages. Colored illustrations. Grades: 5–adult. *Explores the life and work of this great composer. Although written for the older child, the book could easily be used with younger children if an adult discusses the material with them. A time line is included, along with a music glossary.*

BEN'S TRUMPET by Rachel Isadora. New York: Greenwillow Books, 1979. 32 pages. Illustrated. Grades: K–3. *Ben is a black boy who pretends to play the trumpet. When a local jazz musician discovers his desire to play, he takes Ben under his wing. The black-and-white illustrations are in the art-deco style of the twenties. It should be noted, however, that some of the illustrations portray the characters smoking or drinking. (A Caldecott Medal Honor Book, 1980)*

THE BREMEN-TOWN MUSICIANS retold by Ilse Plume. New York: HarperCollins, Trophy, 1987 (originally published in 1980). 30 pages. Colored illustrations. Grades: K–3. *No longer wanted by their masters, a group of animals, one by one, team up to become musicians. On their way to Bremen, the group meets with a band of robbers. Children will enjoy learning how the animals get the best of the robbers and become independent at the same time. (A Caldecott Medal Honor Book, 1981)*

DO YOUR EARS HANG LOW? FIFTY MORE MUSICAL FINGERPLAYS compiled by Tom Glazer. Illustrated by Mila Lazarevich. New York: Doubleday, 1980. 96 pages. Illustrated with music. Grades: Preschool–3. *A collection of fifty wonderful songs. Melodies, piano accompaniments, and guitar chords are provided, as well as instructions for fingerplays to be performed in conjunction with the songs.*

DRUMMER HOFF adapted by Barbara Emberly. Illustrated by Ed Emberly. New York: Simon and Schuster, 1985 (originally published in 1967). 32 pages. Colored illustrations. Grades: Preschool–4. *Here is a story about a cannon being built by many soldiers and a character named Drummer Hoff who fires it off, told in a cumulative style. (Caldecott Medal, 1968)*

EYE WINKER, TOM TINKER, CHIN CHOPPER: FIFTY MUSICAL FINGERPLAYS compiled by Tom Glazer. Illustrated by Ron Himler. New York: Doubleday, Zephyr, 1973. 91 pages. Illustrated with music. Grades: Preschool–3. *Fifty musical fingerplays with piano accompaniments and guitar chords. Directions for the fingerplays are also included.*

FOLLOW THE DRINKING GOURD by Jeanette Winter. New York: Knopf, 1988. 48 pages. Colored illustrations. Grades: K–3. *Peg Leg Joe teaches black slaves the words to the song "Follow the Drinking Gourd." The words, when taken literally, provide directions for escape through the underground railroad. The words and melody are provided at the end.*

FROG WENT A-COURTIN' adapted by John Langstaff. Illustrated by Feodor Rojankovsky. San Diego, Calif.: Harcourt Brace Jovanovich, 1955. 32 pages. Colored illustrations. Grades: Preschool–3. *Based on the 400-year-old song from Scotland, this book depicts the antics of a frog who goes a-courtin'. Langstaff includes a melody at the end. (Caldecott Medal, 1956)*

GERALDINE, THE MUSIC MOUSE by Leo Lionni. New York: Pantheon Books, 1979. 30 pages. Colored illustrations. Grades: Preschool–2. *Geraldine is a mouse who finds a huge piece of cheese. As she starts eating the cheese, she discovers that a statue of a mouse playing a flute is hidden inside. Later that night, the statue introduces Geraldine to the beautiful sounds a flute can produce. Geraldine and her friends eat the statue only after Geraldine has mastered the art of making music herself.*

GO IN AND OUT THE WINDOW: AN ILLUSTRATED SONGBOOK FOR YOUNG PEOPLE by the Metropolitan Museum of Art Staff, musical arrangements and editing by Dan Fox, with commentary by Claude Marks. Illustrations are reproductions of various examples of art. New York: Copublished by the Metropolitan Museum of Art and Henry Holt, 1987. 144 pages. Colored illustrations. Grades: Preschool–adult. *This is by far the most outstanding integration of music and art I have ever seen. Here is a collection of art from the Metropolitan Museum of Art, accompanied by songs on the same subject as the artwork. The music includes lyrics, piano accompaniment, and guitar chords. The commentary explains the music and art. (One of the American Library Association's Notable Books for Children, 1987)*

HILARY KNIGHT'S THE TWELVE DAYS OF CHRISTMAS illustrated by Hilary Knight. New York: Macmillan, Aladdin, 1987. 34 pages. Colored illustrations. Grades: Preschool–3. *A humorous look at the traditional Christmas carol "The Twelve Days of Christmas." By the end of the story, a female bear has received a collection of foxes, pigs, frogs, and other characters, which she transforms into quite a surprise for the true love who sent them to her.*

I KNOW AN OLD LADY WHO SWALLOWED A FLY retold by Nadine Bernard Westcott. Boston: Little, Brown; Joy Street Books, 1980. 34 pages. Colored illustrations. Grades: K–3. *A woman swallows a fly and then a spider and a variety of other creatures. Every page is as much fun as the last. The melody, words, and piano accompaniment can be found on the inside covers of the book.*

THE LITTLE DRUMMER BOY illustrated by Ezra Jack Keats. New York: Macmillan, Collier Books, 1972 (originally pub-

lished in 1968). 33 pages. Colored illustrations. Grades: Preschool–
3. *This picture book is based on the Christmas carol of the same title
by Katherine Davis, Henry Onorati, and Harry Simeone. The Little
Drummer Boy gives the only gift to the Christ Child that he has to
offer: a song on his drum. The unaccompanied melody with words
appears at the back of the book.*

LULLABIES AND NIGHT SONGS arranged by Alec Wilder
and edited by William Engvick. Illustrated by Maurice Sendak. New
York: HarperCollins, 1965. 78 pages. Colored illustrations. Grades:
Preschool–3. *The works of such authors as Robert Louis Stevenson
and Lewis Carroll are set to music by Alec Wilder. The Sendak illustrations are beautiful and add much to this collection. Piano arrangements without chords are included.*

MAKING MUSICAL THINGS: IMPROVISED INSTRU-
MENTS by Ann Wiseman. New York: Macmillan, Scribner Books,
1979. 64 pages. Illustrated. Grades: 2–6. *With this book, children
will enjoy creating their own instruments and then performing on
them. The suggested construction materials can be found around the
house. Some of the projects require adult assistance.*

MAMA DON'T ALLOW: STARRING MILES AND THE
SWAMP BAND adapted by Thacher Hurd. New York: HarperCollins,
1984. 40 pages. Colored illustrations. Grades: Preschool–3. *When
Miles gets a new saxophone, everyone complains that it is too loud.
Miles, however, who is persistent in his practicing, joins others in
forming the Swamp Band, and they are soon asked to play at the
Alligator's Ball. When the band finds that the alligators are planning
to serve them for dinner, the band members use their musical talents
to escape from the situation. Includes music and lyrics.* (Boston
Globe-Horn *Book Award for Best Illustrations, 1985)*

MAX by Rachel Isadora. New York: Macmillan, 1976. 32
pages. Colored illustrations. Grades: Preschool–3. *After walking his
sister to dance class, Max is invited in to participate. The illustrations feature Max in his baseball uniform, dancing with the ballet
students and having a wonderful time.*

MOMMY, BUY ME A CHINA DOLL retold by Harve Ze-
mach. Illustrated by Margot Zemach. New York: Farrar, Straus and
Giroux, Michael di Capua Books, 1975 (originally published in

1966). 32 pages. Colored illustrations. Grades: Preschool–2. *Eliza Lou asks her mother to buy her a china doll. This leads to a wonderful cumulative tale involving the shuffling of people and animals and where they will sleep. The book does not contain the melody to this children's song from the Ozarks, which may be unfamiliar to the reader. (One of the American Library Association's Notable Books for Children, 1966)*

MUSIC, MUSIC FOR EVERYONE by Vera B. Williams. New York: Greenwillow Books, 1984. 32 pages. Colored illustrations. Grades: K–3. *Rosa loves her grandmother very much, but her grandmother is ill and her family is in need of money. Rosa and her friends form the Oak Street Band, and Rosa contributes the money that she has earned from her playing to help with her family's finances. (One of the American Library Association's Notable Books for Children, 1984, and one of the* School Library Journal's *Best Books, 1984) Children will enjoy reading the earlier story about Rosa and her accordion entitled* Something Special for Me.

THE NUTCRACKER by E. T. A. Hoffman and adapted by Janet Schulman. Illustrated by Kay Chorao. New York: Knopf, 1988 (originally published in 1979). 62 pages. Illustrated. Grades: 1–5. *Little does Marie know that her ugly toy nutcracker is really a prince under a magic spell. Children will be excited to hear how Marie comes to his assistance. This version is modeled after the original story (published in 1816). This is a classic story that children look forward to hearing every year. An excellent introduction before viewing the actual ballet, which is also a favorite.*

OLD MACDONALD HAD A FARM retold by Carol Jones. Boston: Houghton Mifflin, 1989. 32 pages. Colored illustrations. Grades: Preschool–2. *A retelling of the story of Old MacDonald, with beautiful illustrations and cut-out pages. This delightful book is perfect for story time.*

PAGES OF MUSIC by Tony Johnston. Illustrated by Tomie De Paola. New York: Putnam, G. P. Putnam's Sons, 1988. 30 pages. Colored illustrations. Grades: K–3. *Paolo is a little boy who visits the island of Sardinia with his mother. He learns to appreciate how the shepherds play the pipes, and he eats* fogli di musica *(pages of music). When Paola grows up, he becomes a composer and conductor. He returns to the island with a special Christmas gift.*

PETER AND THE WOLF adapted from the musical tale by Sergei Prokofiev. Illustrated by Erna Voigt. Boston: David R. Godine, 1987 (originally published in 1980). 32 pages. Colored illustrations. Grades: Preschool–adult. *This is the classic story of Peter, who ignores his grandfather and wanders into the meadow. Other characters include a cat, a duck, a bird, some hunters, and, of course, a wolf which Peter skillfully captures. Not only are the actions in the story portrayed through illustrations, reproductions of the instruments are included, as well as musical motifs.*

THE PHILHARMONIC GETS DRESSED by Karla Kuskin. Illustrated by Marc Simont. New York: HarperCollins, 1982. 42 pages. Colored illustrations. Grades: K–3. *A look at the musicians and the conductor of the Philharmonic Orchestra as they bathe, dress, travel to work, and begin their jobs as performers. (One of the American Library Association's Notable Books for Children, 1982)*

THE RAFFI SINGABLE SONGBOOK by Raffi. Illustrated by Joyce Yamamoto. New York: Crown, 1988 (originally published in 1980). 106 pages. Colored illustrations. Grades: Preschool–6. *Here is a collection of the songs that can be found on Raffi's albums:* Singable Songs for the Very Young, Corner Grocery Store and Other Singable Songs, *and* More Singable Songs. *David Tanner has created delightful arrangements for this collection of children's favorites. Guitar chords are included, along with chord charts for both guitar and ukulele. Illustrations by children are included, along with those of Joyce Yamamoto.*

RONDO IN C by Paul Fleischman. Illustrated by Janet Wentworth. New York: HarperCollins, 1988. 32 pages. Colored illustrations. Grades K–3. *As the main character, a young girl, performs Beethoven's* Rondo in C *at a piano recital, we see through breathtaking illustrations what the audience members are imagining. This would be a wonderful book to read prior to participating in or attending any performance.*

SINGING BEE! A COLLECTION OF FAVORITE CHILDREN'S SONGS compiled by Jane Hart. Illustrated by Anita Lobel. New York: Lothrop, Lee and Shepherd Books, 1989 (originally published in 1982). 160 pages. Colored illustrations. Grades: Preschool–adult. *Includes 125 singing games, fingerplays, lullabies, holiday songs, and more. Piano accompaniments and guitar chords are pro-*

vided. The title index and subject index will be especially useful to teachers. (One of the School Library Journal's *Best Books, 1982)*

SIX LITTLE DUCKS retold by Chris Conover. New York: HarperCollins, Crowell, 1976. 32 pages. Colored illustrations. Grades: Preschool–3. *Based on the children's song by the same title. The illustrations in this book tell more than the words. We see how one duck escorts his friends through quite an adventuresome day. The melody, along with the guitar chords and piano accompaniment, appear at the end of the book.*

SKIP TO MY LOU adapted and illustrated by Nadine Bernard Westcott. Boston: Little, Brown; Joy Street Books, 1989. 32 pages. Colored illustrations. Grades: Preschool–2. *This story begins with a farmer and his wife leaving their son to run the farm. The animals, however, have a completely different idea of who will be in charge. Children will enjoy the frolicking antics of the barnyard creatures. Words, piano accompaniment, and chords are provided for the song.*

SONG AND DANCE MAN by Karen Ackerman. Illustrated by Stephen Gammell. New York: Knopf, 1988. 32 pages. Colored illustrations. Grades: Preschool–3. *A grandfather who shares his talents and vaudeville experiences with his visiting grandchildren. (Caldecott Medal, 1989)*

THE STAR-SPANGLED BANNER illustrated by Peter Spier. New York: Doubleday, 1973. 48 pages. Colored illustrations. Grades: Preschool–adult. *With beautiful illustrations, Spier has brought Francis Scott Key's composition to life. There are historical notes, as well as illustrations of various American flags. Lyrics, piano accompaniment, and guitar chords are included. This is a picture book that all will enjoy.*

THE TRUMPET OF THE SWAN by Elwyn B. White. Illustrated by Edward Frascino. New York: HarperCollins, 1970. 210 pages. Illustrated with music. Grades: 3–6. *Although Louis, a trumpeter swan, has no voice, he learns to do a great many things. One of his accomplishments is being able to play a trumpet that his father has stolen for him. With the help of Sam, a little boy, Louis the Swan is able to restore his father's dignity and to capture the love of another swan. (A finalist for the National Book Award, 1971, and the only*

U.S. book on the Honor List of the International Board on Books for Young People, 1972; Laura Ingalls Wilder Award, 1970; Young Hoosier Award, 1975; William Allen White Children's Book Award, 1973; Sequoyah Children's Book Award, 1973)

WOLFERL: THE FIRST SIX YEARS IN THE LIFE OF WOLFGANG AMADEUS MOZART, 1756–1762 by Lisl Weil. New York: Holiday House, 1991. 32 pages. Colored illustrations. Grades: K–4. *This picture book discusses the life of the young Mozart, including his travels, performances, early compositions, and family. A fine contribution to children's literature.*

YANKEE DOODLE by Edward Bangs. Illustrated by Steven Kellogg. New York: Macmillan, Four Winds Press, 1984. 36 pages. Colored illustrations. Grades: Preschool–3. *Steven Kellogg has turned the song "Yankee Doodle" into a marvelous picture book. The illustrations of a little boy running amid Revolutionary War scenes are sure to capture the young imagination.*

Annotated Discography

This discography includes those recordings that are listed in Part I under "suggested musical resources," as well as in the Subject Guide.

AMERICAN FOLK SONGS FOR CHILDREN sung by Pete Seeger. Folkways Records, 1954. Available on record and cassette, and includes booklet. Grades: K–6. *This collection of songs is a perfect addition to any classroom or home. Includes such favorites as "Bought Me a Cat," "Jim Along Josie," "There Was a Man and He Was Mad," "Clap Your Hands," "She'll Be Coming 'Round the Mountain," "All Around the Kitchen," "Billy Barlow," "Jim Crack Corn," "Train Is A-Coming," "This Old Man,"and "Frog Went A-Courtin'"—all accompanied by five-string banjo. This recording also involves the listener in participatory activities.*

BABY BELUGA sung by Raffi with Ken Whitely. Shoreline, 1980. Available on record (including lyrics), cassette, and CD. Grades: Preschool–1. *Included on this recording are such tunes as "Oats and Beans and Barley," "Day O," "Over in the Meadow," "Kumbaya," as well as original songs by Raffi.*

CORNER GROCERY STORE AND OTHER SINGABLE SONGS sung by Raffi with Ken Whitely. Shoreline, 1979. Available on record (including lyrics), cassette, and CD. Grades: Preschool–5. *Selections include such traditional songs as "Frère Jacques," "Jim*

Along Home," "Pick a Bale O' Cotton," and "Swing Low, Sweet Chariot," plus a variety of original tunes.

FOLLOW THE SUNSET: A BEGINNING GEOGRAPHY RECORD WITH NINE SONGS FROM AROUND THE WORLD sung by Charity Bailey and narrated by Robert Emmett. Adapted for recording by Eunice Holsaert and Charity Bailey. Folkways, 1959. Available on record and includes a booklet with teaching hints, complete narration, and song lyrics. Grades: K–3. *As the listener travels around the world through song, lullabies from various geographical areas are introduced. Most of the songs are in English. This recording does an excellent job of integrating music, geography, and astronomy.*

INVITATION TO MUSIC prepared and narrated by Elie Siegmeister. Folkways Records, 1961. Available on record and includes a booklet with musical examples. Grades 3–6. *Introduces musical concepts through exceptional examples of music by such composers as Beethoven and Schubert. Also included are samples of folk music, jazz, and music from various countries. This recording is geared for the older child. The book by the same title, also by Elie Siegmeister, was out of print at the time of this publication but is another wonderful resource if it can be obtained.*

LULLABIES FROM 'ROUND THE WORLD sung by Marilyn Horne and Richard Robinson. Settings by Ruth White. Rhythms Productions, 1956. Available on record and includes lyrics. Grades: Preschool–1. *A collection of lullabies from around the world. Countries that are represented include Japan, China, Scotland, and Germany, among others.*

PLAY YOUR INSTRUMENTS AND MAKE A PRETTY SOUND sung by Ella Jenkins with Franz Jackson and his Original Jazz All-Stars. Folkways, 1968. Available on record (including words and narrative) and cassette. Grades: Preschool–adult. *Various styles of music are demonstrated by a jazz band as the children are invited to clap, march, sing, and listen to instruments. The group consists of a trumpet, trombone, clarinet, drums, tuba, drum, banjo, as well as a ukulele and a harmonica.*

PUEBLO INDIANS IN STORY, SONG, AND DANCE performed by Swift Eagle. Caedmon, 1972. Available on cassette.

Grades: 4–6. *The songs and dances performed on this recording tell of the legends and beliefs of the Pueblo Indians. An excellent resource when studying Native Americans.*

RHYTHMS OF CHILDHOOD sung by Ella Jenkins. Folkways, 1963. Available on record and includes a booklet with teaching suggestions for percussion activities. Grades: Preschool–adult. *A great collection of songs about nature which involves the listener in participatory activities. A variety of instruments form the accompaniment to these selections. Rhythms from other countries are featured.*

RISE AND SHINE sung by Raffi with Ken Whitely. Shoreline, 1982. Available on record (including lyrics), cassette, and CD. Grades: Preschool–5. *Seventeen children's songs are featured on this recording, including "He's Got the Whole World in His Hands," "The Wheels on the Bus," and "Thumbelina." Raffi is accompanied by a group of children on a number of selections, and there is a variety of instrumental scoring.*

SING CHILDREN SING: SONGS OF MEXICO performed by the Ninos Cantores de la Ciudad de Mexico and Orchestra and arranged and conducted by Sergio Andrade. Caedmon, 1980. Available on record (including bilingual lyrics) and cassette. Grades: K–adult. *This collection of Mexican folk songs is particularly appealing because the selections are performed by children in Spanish. Other recordings in this series each feature songs from a different country.*

SING CHILDREN SING: SONGS OF THE UNITED STATES OF AMERICA performed by the New York City Opera Children's Chorus and arranged and conducted by Robert DeCormier. Caedmon, 1977. Available on cassette. Grades: Preschool–6. *Various sections of the United States are represented in this collection of folk songs. Includes such standards as "Go Tell Aunt Rhody," "Shenandoah," "The Erie Canal," and "Simple Gifts."*

SINGABLE SONGS FOR THE VERY YOUNG sung by Raffi with Ken Whitely. Shoreline, 1976. Available on record, cassette, and CD, and includes lyrics. Grades: Preschool–1. *All types of songs are included, such as "Spider on the Floor," "Baa Baa Black Sheep," "Five Little Frogs," and "I Wonder If I'm Growing." This recording also features the voices of children, which is sure to motivate the young singer.*

SOUND EFFECTS collected by World Music Service. Gateway Records, R. T. V. Communications. Cassettes, 1979; CDs released in 1992. Grades: Preschool–adult. *Gateway has produced a series of recordings each featuring realistic sound effects. A wonderful way of introducing children to the multitude of sounds that surround us.*

WEE SING SING-ALONGS by Pamela Conn Beall and Susan Hagen Nipp. Price/Stern/Sloan, 1990. Available on cassette and includes songbook. Grades: Preschool–3. *This collection of folk songs, spirituals, and rounds is sure to please children. The songbook that is included contains melodies, lyrics, and guitar chords.*

YOU'LL SING A SONG AND I'LL SING A SONG performed by Ella Jenkins and the Urban Gateways Children's Chorus. Folkways Records, 1966. Available on record (including a booklet) and cassette. Grades: Preschool–2. *Includes such tunes as "This Train," "Miss Mary Mack," and "Did You Feed My Cow?" Children will enjoy singing along with the young performers on the first side of the recording. The second side features instrumental versions of the same selections so that children may create their own lyrics.*

ADDITIONAL RECORDINGS

The following classical pieces may be used in a variety of ways. Recordings of these should be easily obtainable through your public library system.

- *Carnival of the Animals* by Camille Saint-Saëns
- *Danse Macabre* by Camille Saint-Saëns
- *The Fantastic Toyshop* by Gioacchino Rossini
- *Hansel and Gretel* by Engelbert Humperdinck
- *Mother Goose Suite* by Maurice Ravel
- *Night on Bald Mountain* by Modest Mussorgsky
- *Nutcracker Suite* by Peter Tchaikovsky
- *Peer Gynt Suite* by Edvard Grieg
- *Peter and the Wolf* by Sergei Prokofiev
- *Sorcerer's Apprentice* by Paul Dukas
- *The Young Person's Guide to the Orchestra* by Benjamin Britten

Appendix: Subject Guide

FOR THOSE TEACHERS AND PARENTS WHO WANT TO INTEGRATE music with various topics that are being covered in the classroom or that are of particular interest to the individual child, this subject guide will prove useful. The abbreviation that follows each title indicates whether it falls under the category of general literature for children (GL), musical literature for children (ML), or a recording (R). Feel free to use these books and recordings to introduce any other subjects that may come to mind.

ANIMALS AND OTHER LIVING CREATURES

ALLIGATORS
Mama Don't Allow: Starring Miles and the Swamp Band (ML)
BEARS
Brown Bear, Brown Bear, What Do You See? (GL)
Hilary Knight's The Twelve Days of Christmas (ML)
CATS
Millions of Cats (GL)
CHICKENS
Chickens Aren't the Only Ones (GL)
The Little Red Hen (GL)
DUCKS
Six Little Ducks (ML)
FROGS AND TOADS
Frog and Toad Are Friends (GL)
Frog Went A-Courtin' (ML)
INSECTS
Charlotte's Web (spiders) (GL)
I Know an Old Lady Who Swallowed a Fly (flies and spiders) (ML)

James and the Giant Peach: A Children's Story (various kinds)
(GL)
The Very Hungry Caterpillar (caterpillars/butterflies) (GL)
Why Mosquitoes Buzz in People's Ears: A West African Tale
(mosquitoes) (GL)
MICE
Geraldine, the Music Mouse (ML)
MONKEYS
*Caps for Sale: A Tale of a Peddler, Some Monkeys, and Their
Monkey Business* (GL)
PIGS
Charlotte's Web (GL)
POSSUMS
Mama Don't Allow: Starring Miles and the Swamp Band (ML)
RABBITS
Goodnight Moon (GL)
The Tale of Peter Rabbit (GL)
The Velveteen Rabbit (GL)
Who's in Rabbit's House? A Masai Tale (GL)
SWANS
The Trumpet of the Swan (ML)
TIGERS
Leo the Late Bloomer (GL)
VARIOUS TYPES
The Bremen-Town Musicians (ML)
Brown Bear, Brown Bear, What Do You See? (GL)
I Know an Old Lady Who Swallowed a Fly (ML)
WOLVES
Peter and the Wolf (ML)

ART

*Go In and Out the Window: An Illustrated Songbook for Young
People* (various styles) (ML)

BEHAVIOR

CARELESSNESS
Strega Nona's Magic Lessons (GL)
MISBEHAVIOR
Charlie and the Chocolate Factory (GL)
The Tale of Peter Rabbit (GL)
Where the Wild Things Are: 25th Anniversary Edition (GL)

CAREERS

MUSICIANS
The Philharmonic Gets Dressed (ML)
PEDDLERS
*Caps for Sale: A Tale of a Peddler, Some Monkeys, and Their
Monkey Business* (GL)

CLOTHING

*Caps for Sale: A Tale of a Peddler, Some Monkeys, and Their
Monkey Business* (GL)
The Philharmonic Gets Dressed (ML)

COLORS

Brown Bear, Brown Bear, What Do You See? (GL)

COMPOSERS

America, I Hear You: A Story About George Gershwin (ML)
Beethoven (ML)
*Wolferl: The First Six Years in the Life of Wolfgang Amadeus
Mozart, 1756–1762* (ML)

COOPERATION

Charlotte's Web (GL)

CULTURAL/ETHNIC STUDIES

AFRICAN
Rhythms of Childhood (R)
Who's in Rabbit's House? A Masai Tale (GL)
Why Mosquitoes Buzz in People's Ears: A West African Tale (GL)
AFRO-AMERICAN
*All Night, All Day: A Child's First Book of African-American
Spirituals* (ML)
Ben's Trumpet (ML)
Black Is Brown Is Tan (GL)
Follow the Drinking Gourd (ML)
The Snowy Day (GL)

CHINESE
  Chinese New Year (GL)
  Ming Lo Moves the Mountain (GL)
FRENCH
  Corner Grocery Store and Other Singable Songs (R)
ITALIAN
  Strega Nona's Magic Lessons (GL)
JEWISH
  A Picture Book of Jewish Holidays (GL)
MEXICAN
  All of You Was Singing (Aztec Indians) (ML)
  Sing Children Sing: Songs of Mexico (R)
NATIVE AMERICAN (AMERICAN INDIAN)
  American Indian Music and Musical Instruments (ML)
  From Abenaki to Zuni: A Dictionary of Native American Tribes
    (GL)
  Pueblo Indians in Story, Song, and Dance (R)
  Small Wolf (GL)
OTHERS
  Follow the Sunset: A Beginning Geography Record with Nine
    Songs from Around the World (R)
  Lullabies from 'Round the World (R)
  Miss Rumphius (GL)
  Pages of Music (ML)

CUMULATIVE TALES

  Drummer Hoff (ML)
  Hilary Knight's The Twelve Days of Christmas (ML)
  I Know an Old Lady Who Swallowed a Fly (ML)
  Mommy, Buy Me a China Doll (ML)
  Too Much Noise (GL)
  Why Mosquitoes Buzz in People's Ears: A West African Tale (GL)

DAYS OF THE WEEK

  The Very Hungry Caterpillar (GL)

DANCE

BALLET
  Max (ML)

FOLK DANCE
Barn Dance! (ML)
VAUDEVILLE
Song and Dance Man (ML)

DWELLINGS

ALL TYPES
A House Is a House for Me (GL)
HOUSES
Ming Lo Moves the Mountain (GL)
FARMS
Charlotte's Web (GL)

FAIRY TALES AND FOLKTALES

AFRICAN
Who's in Rabbit's House? A Masai Tale (GL)
Why Mosquitoes Buzz in People's Ears: A West African Tale (GL)
GERMAN
The Bremen-Town Musicians (ML)
MEXICAN
All of You Was Singing (Aztec Indians) (ML)
RUSSIAN
The Nutcracker (ML)
Peter and the Wolf (ML)

FAMILIES

AUNTS
James and the Giant Peach: A Children's Story (GL)
Miss Rumphius (GL)
FATHERS/SONS
Danny, the Champion of the World (GL)
GRANDFATHERS
Song and Dance Man (ML)
GRANDMOTHERS
Music, Music for Everyone (ML)
INTERRACIAL
Black Is Brown Is Tan (GL)

MOTHERS/DAUGHTERS
　The Quilt Story (GL)

FANTASY

　Charlie and the Chocolate Factory (GL)
　Charlotte's Web (GL)
　James and the Giant Peach: A Children's Story (GL)
　The Little Prince (GL)
　The Trumpet of the Swan (ML)
　The Velveteen Rabbit (GL)
　Where the Wild Things Are: 25th Anniversary Edition (GL)

FRIENDSHIP

　Charlotte's Web (GL)
　A Friend Is Someone Who Likes You: Silver Anniversary Edition
　　(GL)
　Frog and Toad Are Friends (GL)
　The Little Red Hen (GL)
　Miss Rumphius (GL)

GEOGRAPHY

　*Follow the Sunset: A Beginning Geography Record with Nine
　　Songs from Around the World* (R)

GROWING UP

　Leo the Late Bloomer (GL)

HISTORY

CALIFORNIA
　If You Lived at the Time of the Great San Francisco Earthquake
　　(GL)
UNITED STATES
　Follow the Drinking Gourd (slavery) (ML)
　If You Sailed on the Mayflower (GL)
　The Star-Spangled Banner (War of 1812) (ML)
　Yankee Doodle (Revolution, 1775–83) (ML)

HOLIDAYS

CHINESE NEW YEAR
  Chinese New Year (GL)
CHRISTMAS
  Hilary Knight's The Twelve Days of Christmas (ML)
  The Little Drummer Boy (ML)
  The Nutcracker (ML)
  Pages of Music (ML)
  The Polar Express (GL)
  The Velveteen Rabbit (GL)
EASTER
  The Tale of Peter Rabbit (GL)
FOURTH OF JULY
  The Star-Spangled Banner (ML)
  Yankee Doodle (ML)
HALLOWEEN
  It's Halloween (GL)
  Where the Wild Things Are: 25th Anniversary Edition (GL)
OTHERS
  A Picture Book of Jewish Holidays (GL)
THANKSGIVING
  If You Sailed on the Mayflower (GL)

HUMOR

  Caps for Sale: A Tale of a Peddler, Some Monkeys, and Their Monkey Business (GL)
  Charlie and the Chocolate Factory (GL)
  Danny, the Champion of the World (GL)
  The New Kid on the Block (GL)
  Strega Nona's Magic Lessons (GL)

INSTRUMENTS

CONSTRUCTION
  American Indian Music and Musical Instruments (ML)
  Making Musical Things: Improvised Instruments (ML)
RHYTHM INSTRUMENT ACTIVITIES
  Play Your Instruments and Make a Pretty Sound (R)
  Rhythms of Childhood (R)

INTERDEPENDENCE

The Little Red Hen (GL)

MAGIC

James and the Giant Peach: A Children's Story (GL)
Strega Nona's Magic Lessons (GL)
The Velveteen Rabbit (GL)

MATH

Hilary Knight's The Twelve Days of Christmas (ML)
Millions of Cats (GL)

MONSTERS

Where the Wild Things Are: 25th Anniversary Edition (GL)

MOVEMENT ACTIVITIES

American Folk Songs for Children (R)
Play Your Instruments and Make a Pretty Sound (R)

MOVING

Ming Lo Moves the Mountain (GL)
The Quilt Story (GL)

MUSIC APPRECIATION AND CONCEPTS

Invitation to Music (R)
Play Your Instruments and Make a Pretty Sound (R)
Rhythms of Childhood (R)
Rondo in C (ML)
You'll Sing a Song and I'll Sing a Song (R)

MUSICAL STYLES

*All Night, All Day: A Child's First Book of African-American
   Spirituals* (spirituals) (ML)

Barn Dance! (country) (ML)
Ben's Trumpet (jazz) (ML)
Follow the Sunset: A Beginning Geography Record with Nine Songs from Around the World (lullabies) (R)
Go In and Out the Window: An Illustrated Songbook for Young People (various styles) (ML)
Invitation to Music (various styles) (R)
Lullabies and Night Songs (lullabies) (ML)
Lullabies from 'Round the World (lullabies) (R)
Play Your Instruments and Make a Pretty Sound (various styles) (R)
Rondo in C (classical) (ML)
Singing Bee! A Collection of Favorite Children's Songs (various styles) (ML)
Song and Dance Man (vaudeville) (ML)
The Star-Spangled Banner (patriotic) (ML)
The Trumpet of the Swan (various styles) (ML)
Yankee Doodle (patriotic) (ML)

MUSICIANS

Ben's Trumpet (ML)
The Bremen-Town Musicians (ML)
Drummer Hoff (ML)
Geraldine, the Music Mouse (ML)
The Little Drummer Boy (ML)
Mama Don't Allow: Starring Miles and the Swamp Band (ML)
Music, Music for Everyone (ML)
Pages of Music (ML)
The Philharmonic Gets Dressed (ML)
Rondo in C (ML)
The Trumpet of the Swan (ML)

NATURE AND SCIENCE

ASTRONOMY
   Follow the Sunset: A Beginning Geography Record with Nine Songs from Around the World (R)
EARTHQUAKES
   If You Lived at the Time of the Great San Francisco Earthquake (GL)

ENVIRONMENTAL STUDIES
  Rhythms of Childhood (R)
  Sound Effects (R)
METAMORPHOSIS
  The Very Hungry Caterpillar (GL)
NIGHT
  Goodnight Moon (GL)
OVIPAROUS CREATURES
  Chickens Aren't the Only Ones (GL)
PLANTS
  The Little Red Hen (grain) (GL)
  Miss Rumphius (flowers) (GL)
  The Very Hungry Caterpillar (GL)
SEASONS AND WEATHER
  The Sky Is Full of Song (GL)
  The Snowy Day (GL)

ORCHESTRAS/BANDS

  Mama Don't Allow: Starring Miles and the Swamp Band (ML)
  Music, Music for Everyone (ML)
  Pages of Music (ML)
  Peter and the Wolf (ML)
  The Philharmonic Gets Dressed (ML)

PARTICIPATION

  Brown Bear, Brown Bear, What Do You See? (GL)
  The Little Red Hen (GL)

POETRY AND RHYME

COLLECTIONS
  It's Halloween (GL)
  The New Kid on the Block (GL)
  *The Random House Book of Mother Goose: A Treasury of 306
    Timeless Nursery Rhymes* (GL)
  Sing a Song of Popcorn: Every Child's Book of Poems (GL)
  The Sky Is Full of Song (GL)
BOOKS IN RHYME
  Black Is Brown Is Tan (GL)
  Brown Bear, Brown Bear, What Do You See? (GL)

Chicken's Aren't the Only Ones (GL)
Goodnight Moon (GL)
A House Is a House for Me (GL)

PROBLEM SOLVING

Who's in Rabbit's House? A Masai Tale (GL)

QUILTS

The Quilt Story (GL)

REPETITION

Brown Bear, Brown Bear, What Do You See? (GL)
Chickens Aren't the Only Ones (GL)
Drummer Hoff (ML)
Millions of Cats (GL)
Too Much Noise (GL)
Who's in Rabbit's House? A Masai Tale (GL)

RHYME. SEE POETRY AND RHYME

SEQUENCING

*Caps for Sale: A Tale of a Peddler, Some Monkeys, and Their
    Monkey Business* (GL)
Hilary Knight's The Twelve Days of Christmas (ML)
Millions of Cats (GL)

SONGS

CHILDREN'S SONGS AND SINGING GAMES
  American Folk Songs for Children (R)
  *American Folk Songs for Children in Home, School, and Nursery
    School: A Book for Children, Parents, and Teachers* (ML)
  Baby Beluga (R)
  Corner Grocery Store and Other Singable Songs (R)
  Do Your Ears Hang Low? Fifty More Musical Fingerplays (ML)
  *Eye Winker, Tom Tinker, Chin Chopper: Fifty Musical
    Fingerplays* (ML)

*Go In and Out the Window: An Illustrated Songbook for Young
People* (ML)
I Know an Old Lady Who Swallowed a Fly (ML)
Lullabies and Night Songs (ML)
Old MacDonald Had a Farm (ML)
The Raffi Singable Songbook (ML)
Rise and Shine (R)
Singable Songs for the Very Young (R)
Singing Bee! A Collection of Favorite Children's Songs (ML)
Six Little Ducks (ML)
You'll Sing a Song and I'll Sing a Song (R)

FOLK SONGS

*All Night, All Day: A Child's First Book of African-American
Spirituals* (ML)
American Folk Songs for Children (American) (R)
*American Folk Songs for Children in Home, School, and Nursery
School: A Book for Children, Parents, and Teachers* (American)
(ML)
Corner Grocery Store and Other Singable Songs (American and
French) (R)
*Follow the Sunset: A Beginning Geography Record with Nine
Songs from Around the World* (Others) (R)
Frog Went A-Courtin' (Scottish) (ML)
Mommy, Buy Me a China Doll (American) (ML)
Old MacDonald Had a Farm (American) (ML)
Rise and Shine (American) (R)
Sing Children Sing: Songs of Mexico (Mexican) (R)
Sing Children Sing: Songs of the United States of America
(American) (R)
Skip to My Lou (American) (ML)
Wee Sing Sing-Alongs (American) (R)

PICTURE BOOKS BASED ON SONGS

The Bremen-Town Musicians (ML)
Follow the Drinking Gourd (ML)
Frog Went A-Courtin' (ML)
Hilary Knight's The Twelve Days of Christmas (ML)
I Know an Old Lady Who Swallowed a Fly (ML)
The Little Drummer Boy (ML)
Mama Don't Allow: Starring Miles and the Swamp Band (ML)
Mommy, Buy Me a China Doll (ML)
Old MacDonald Had a Farm (ML)
Six Little Ducks (ML)

Skip to My Lou (ML)
The Star-Spangled Banner (ML)
Yankee Doodle (ML)
ROUNDS
    Wee Sing Sing-Alongs (R)

SOUND EFFECTS

Sound Effects (R)

SPORTS

BASEBALL
    Max (ML)

TOYS

Mommy, Buy Me a China Doll (ML)
The Nutcracker (ML)
The Velveteen Rabbit (GL)

TRAINS

The Polar Express (GL)

Glossary of Musical Terms

Accompaniment. The rhythmic and harmonic musical parts that underlie the melody.

Aerophone. An instrument that requires air in order to produce a tone.

Ballad. A particular type of folk song that tells a story.

Barred instrument. An instrument, such as a xylophone or glockenspiel, that has pitch-producing tone bars.

Beat. The steady pulse of music.

Brass instrument. An instrument in a Western symphony orchestra, such as a trombone, trumpet, or tuba, that is made of brass and has a conical or cup mouthpiece.

Chordophone. An instrument that may produce more than one tone at the same time.

Choreography. The steps and movements of a dance.

Chorus. A group of singers or speakers performing at the same time; the refrain of a song.

Duet. Two musicians performing the same composition simultaneously; a composition written for two musicians.

Duration. The period during which music moves through time. May encompass rhythm, beat, and meter.

Dynamics. The degrees of loudness or softness.

Electronic instrument. An instrument powered by electricity.

Elements. The rudiments of music such as dynamics, tempo, melody, harmony, duration, texture, timbre, and form.

Folk song. A song that is associated with a specific country, region, or cultural group.

Form. The way in which parts of a composition are organized or structured.

Harmony. A combination of tones of different pitches performed at the same time.

Idiophone. An instrument that resonates.

Lullaby. A song used to lull children to sleep.

Melodic contour. The shape (rise and fall) of a melodic line.

Melodic pattern. A specific combination of pitches that produces a sequence which may repeat.

Melody. Successive tones in a vocal line or instrumental line.

Membranophone. A percussion instrument that has a stretched skin, such as a drum.

Meter. The way that musical notation is measured in groups of pulses between the bar lines.

Musical genre. A song or composition based on a specific form, content, or style.

Notation. A system of symbols and signs for communicating musical ideas.

Note. A symbol that expresses a pitch and duration of a musical tone.

Ostinato. A melodic or rhythmic pattern that is repetitive.

Patriotic song. A song that speaks of patriotism or that was written as part of a significant historical event.

Percussion instrument. An instrument that is struck or hit. Also called a rhythm instrument.

Phrase. A musical statement, comparable to a phrase or clause in a sentence.

Pitch. The highness or lowness of a tone.

Quartet. Four musicians performing the same composition simultaneously; a composition written for four musicians.

Rest. A symbol that expresses a duration of silence.

Rhythm. The length of sounds and silences.

Rhythmic pattern. A combination of long sounds, short sounds, and/or rests arranged in a specific pattern, which may repeat.

Rhythm instrument. An instrument that is struck or hit. Also called a percussion instrument.

Rote instruction. Teaching music without the use of written notation.

Round. A song in which voices enter in turn, and return to the beginning upon reaching the end.

Section. A separate portion of a composition; an instrumental or vocal section in a performing group, such as the woodwind section or string section.

Solo. One musician performing a composition; a composition written for one musician.

String instrument. An instrument found in a Western symphony orchestra and played with a bow, such as a violin or viola. May also refer to any instrument that possesses strings.

Style. The unique way in which musical elements are combined to produce music characteristic of historical periods and cultures. Examples include baroque, classical, and romantic.

Tempo. The speed of music.

Texture. The complexity or simplicity of a composition; the aural effect using combinations of sounds, as with different instruments, to produce thin or thick sound qualities.

Timbre. The unique characteristic of a voice or instrument.

Tone color. The timbre of a voice or instrument; a bright or dark effect.

Trio. Three musicians performing the same composition simultaneously; a composition written for three musicians.

Woodwind instrument. An instrument found in a Western symphony orchestra that requires air to create vibrations through reeds or in passing over an opening such as on a flute.

References

BOOKS AND ARTICLES FOR ADULTS

Anderson, William M., and Joy E. Lawrence. "Approaches to Allied Arts." *Music Educator's Journal* 69, no. 1 (September 1982): 31–35.

Bowker, R. R. *Children's Books in Print.* New Providence, N.J.: Bowker, 1991.

Cardarelli, Aldo F. *Twenty-One Ways to Use Music in Teaching the Language Arts.* Evansville: Indiana State University, 1979. (ERIC Document Reproduction Service No. ED 176 268)

Children's Book Council. *Children's Books: Awards and Prizes.* New York: Children's Book Council, 1986.

Corseri, Gary Steven. "To Teach Poetry, Start with a Song." *Learning* 10, no. 8 (March 1982): 90.

Donlan, Dan. "Music and the Language Arts Curriculum." *English Journal* 63, no. 7 (October 1974): 86–88.

Gillespie, John T., and Corinne J. Naden. *Best Books for Children: Preschool Through Grade Six,* 4th edition. New York: Bowker, 1990.

Kaplan, Don. "Music in the Classroom: A New Approach." *Learning* 13, no. 5 (January 1985): 28–31.

Lamme, Linda Leonard. "Song Picture Books—A Maturing Genre of Children's Literature." *Language Arts* 56, no. 4 (April 1979): 400–407.

Lee, Lauren K., ed. *The Elementary School Library Collection: A Guide to Books and Other Media, Phases 1-2-3.* Williamsport, Pa.: Brodart, 1992.

Livo, Norma J. "Multiply Music with Books and Add Art." *Elementary English* 52, no. 4 (April 1975): 541–44.

Schmidt, Lloyd. "Music as a Learning Mode." *Music Educator's Journal* 63, no. 1 (September 1976): 94–97.

Shaffer, Glenis T. "Music Teaches Poetry, Poetry Teaches Music." *Music Educator's Journal* 69, no. 1 (September 1982): 40–42.

Smardo, Francis A. "Using Children's Literature as a Prelude or Finale to Music Experiences with Young Children." *The Reading Teacher* 37, no. 8 (April 1984): 700–705.

Stecher, Miriam B. "Music All Day Long." *Parents Magazine* 60, no. 6 (June 1985): 68–74.

Stover, Lois T. "Read a Book for Music Class? Are You Serious?" *Music Educator's Journal* 76, no. 2 (October 1989): 48–52.

Taylor, Gail Cohen. "ERIC/RCS Report: Music in Language Arts Instruction." *Language Arts* 58, no. 3 (March 1981): 363–67.

Trade Service Corporation. *Phonolog Reports*. San Diego, Calif.: Trade Service Corporation, 1992.

Warner, Laverne. "37 Music Ideas for the Nonmusical Teacher." *Childhood Education* 58, no. 3 (January/February 1982): 134–37.

Werner, Peter H., ed. "Movement, Music, and Children's Literature." *Physical Education* 31, no. 4 (December 1974): 216–18.

Wright, Stephanie Gerjovich. *Music: A Vehicle for Teaching Certain Aspects of the Elementary Language Arts*. Paper presented at the Annual Meeting of the National Council of Teachers of English, New York, N.Y., November 1977. (ERIC Document Reproduction Service No. ED 150 599)

―――. *Music, Songs, & Literature*. Paper presented at the Annual Meeting of the National Council of Teachers of English, San Francisco, California, November 1979. (ERIC Document Reproduction Service No. ED 181 480)

Other Interesting Reading for Adults

California State Department of Education. *The California Visual and Performing Arts Framework*. Sacramento, 1989.

―――. *Recommended Readings in Literature: Kindergarten through Grade Eight*. Sacramento, 1988.

———. *Recommended Readings in Literature: Kindergarten through Grade Eight: Addendum*. Sacramento, 1990.

Chocksy, Lois, and Robert M. Abramson, Avon E. Gillespie, and David Woods. *Teaching Music in the Twentieth Century*. New Jersey: Prentice-Hall, 1986.

Fleischman, Paul. "Sound and Sense." *The Horn Book Magazine* 62, no. 5 (September/October 1986): 551–55.

Gingrich, D. *Relating the Arts*. New York: Center for Applied Research in Education, 1974.

Judy, Stephanie. *Making Music for the Joy of It: Enhancing Creativity, Skills, and Musical Confidence*. Los Angeles: Jeremy P. Tarcher, 1990.

Mann, Raymond E. *The Effect of Music and Sound Effects on the Listening Comprehension of Fourth Grade Students*. Paper presented at the Annual Convention of the Association for Educational Communications and Technology. New Orleans, Louisiana, March 1979. (ERIC Document Reproduction Service No. ED 172 738).

Markel, Roberta. *Music for Your Child: A Complete Guide for Parents and Teachers*. New York: Facts on File, 1983.

Painter, William M. *Musical Story Hours: Using Music With Storytelling and Puppetry*. Hamden, Conn.: Library Professional Publications, 1989.

Trelease, Jim. *The Read-Aloud Handbook*. New York: Penguin, 1985.

Upitis, Rena. *A Child's Development of Music Notation through Composition: A Case Study*. Paper presented at the Annual Meeting of the American Educational Research Association, Washington, D.C., April 1987. (ERIC Document Reproduction Service No. ED 284 780)

BOOKS FOR CHILDREN

Aardema, Verna. *Who's in Rabbit's House? A Masai Tale*. New York: Dial, 1977.

———. *Why Mosquitoes Buzz in People's Ears: A West African Tale*. New York: Dial, 1975.

Ackerman, Karen. *Song and Dance Man*. New York: Knopf, 1988.

Adler, David. *A Picture Book of Jewish Holidays*. New York: Holiday House, 1981.

Adoff, Arnold. *Black Is Brown Is Tan*. New York: HarperCollins, 1973.

Anglund, Joan Walsh. *A Friend Is Someone Who Likes You: Silver Anniversary Edition*. San Diego, Calif.: Harcourt Brace Jovanovich, 1983.

Benchley, Nathaniel. *Small Wolf*. New York: HarperCollins, 1972.

Blackwood, Alan. *Beethoven*. New York: Franklin-Watts, Bookwright, 1987.

Brown, Margaret Wise. *Goodnight Moon*. New York: HarperCollins, 1947.

Brown, Tricia. *Chinese New Year*. New York: Henry Holt, 1987.

Bryan, Ashley. *All Night, All Day: A Child's First Book of African-American Spirituals*. New York: Macmillan, Atheneum, 1991.

Carle, Eric. *The Very Hungry Caterpillar*. New York: Putnam, Philomel, 1981.

Conover, Chris. *Six Little Ducks*. New York: HarperCollins, Crowell, 1976.

Cooney, Barbara. *Miss Rumphius*. New York: Viking Children's Books, 1982.

Dahl, Roald. *Charlie and the Chocolate Factory*. New York: Knopf, 1991.

————. *Danny, the Champion of the World*. New York: Knopf, 1975.

————. *James and the Giant Peach: A Children's Story*. New York: Knopf, 1962.

De Paola, Tomie. *Strega Nona's Magic Lessons*. San Diego, Calif.: Harcourt Brace Jovanovich, 1982.

De Regniers, Beatrice Schenk, et al. *Sing a Song of Popcorn: Every Child's Book of Poems*. New York: Scholastic, Scholastic Hardcover, 1988.

Emberly, Barbara. *Drummer Hoff*. New York: Simon and Schuster, 1985.

Fichter, George S. *American Indian Music and Musical Instruments*. New York: David McKay, 1978.

Fleischman, Paul. *Rondo in C*. New York: HarperCollins, 1988.

Gag, Wanda. *Millions of Cats*. New York: Putnam, Coward-McCann, 1977.

Galdone, Paul. *The Little Red Hen*. Boston: Houghton Mifflin, Clarion Books, 1979.

Glazer, Tom. *Do Your Ears Hang Low? Fifty More Musical Fingerplays*. New York: Doubleday, 1980.

———. *Eye Winker, Tom Tinker, Chin Chopper: Fifty Musical Fingerplays*. New York: Doubleday, Zephyr, 1973.

Hart, Jane. *Singing Bee! A Collection of Favorite Children's Songs*. New York: Lothrop, Lee and Shepherd Books, 1989.

Heller, Ruth. *Chickens Aren't the Only Ones*. New York: Putnam, Grosset and Dunlap, 1981.

Hoberman, Mary Ann. *A House Is a House for Me*. New York: Viking Children's Books, 1978.

Hopkins, Lee Bennett. *The Sky Is Full of Song*. New York: HarperCollins, 1983.

Hurd, Thacher. *Mama Don't Allow: Starring Miles and the Swamp Band*. New York: HarperCollins, 1984.

Isadora, Rachel. *Ben's Trumpet*. New York: Greenwillow Books, 1979.

———. *Max*. New York: Macmillan, 1976.

Johnston, Tony. *Pages of Music*. New York: Putnam, G. P. Putnam's Sons, 1988.

———. *The Quilt Story*. New York: Putnam, G. P. Putnam's Sons, 1985.

Jones, Carol. *Old MacDonald Had a Farm*. Boston: Houghton Mifflin, 1989.

Keats, Ezra Jack. *The Little Drummer Boy*. New York: Macmillan, Collier Books, 1972.

———. *The Snowy Day*. New York: Viking Children's Books, 1962.

Kellogg, Steven. *Yankee Doodle*. New York: Macmillan, Four Winds Press, 1984.

Knight, Hilary. *Hilary Knight's The Twelve Days of Christmas*. New York: Macmillan, Aladdin, 1987.

Kraus, Robert. *Leo the Late Bloomer*. New York: HarperCollins, Crowell, 1971.

Kuskin, Karla. *The Philharmonic Gets Dressed*. New York: HarperCollins, 1982.

Langstaff, John. *Frog Went A-Courtin'*. San Diego, Calif.: Harcourt Brace Jovanovich, 1955.

Levine, Ellen. *If You Lived at the Time of the Great San Francisco Earthquake*. New York: Scholastic, 1987.

Lewis, Richard. *All of You Was Singing*. New York: Macmillan, Atheneum, 1991.

Lionni, Leo. *Geraldine, the Music Mouse*. New York: Pantheon Books, 1979.

Lobel, Arnold. *Frog and Toad Are Friends*. New York: HarperCollins, 1970.

———. *Ming Lo Moves the Mountain*. New York: Greenwillow Books, 1982.

———. *The Random House Book of Mother Goose: A Treasury of 306 Timeless Nursery Rhymes*. New York: Random House, Random Juvenial, 1986.

Martin, Bill, Jr. *Brown Bear, Brown Bear, What Do You See?* New York: Henry Holt, 1983.

Martin, Bill, Jr., and John Archambault. *Barn Dance!* New York: Henry Holt, 1986.

McGovern, Ann. *If You Sailed on the Mayflower*. New York: Scholastic, 1985.

———. *Too Much Noise*. Boston: Houghton Mifflin, 1967.

Metropolitan Museum of Art Staff. *Go In and Out the Window: An Illustrated Songbook for Young People*. New York: Copublished by the Metropolitan Museum of Art and Henry Holt, 1987.

Mitchell, Barbara. *America, I Hear You: A Story About George Gershwin*. Minneapolis: Carolrhoda Books, 1987.

Nichols, Janet. *Women Music Makers*. New York: Walker, 1992.

Plume, Ilse. *The Bremen-Town Musicians*. New York: HarperCollins, Trophy, 1987.

Potter, Beatrix. *The Tale of Peter Rabbit*. New York: Frederick Warne, 1987.

Prelutsky, Jack. *It's Halloween*. New York: Greenwillow Books, 1977.

———. *The New Kid on the Block*. New York: Greenwillow Books, 1984.

Raffi. *The Raffi Singable Songbook*. New York: Crown, 1988.

Saint-Exupery, Antoine de. *The Little Prince*. San Diego, Calif.: Harcourt Brace Jovanovich, 1943.

Schulman, Janet, and E. T. A. Hoffman. *The Nutcracker*. New York: Knopf, 1988.

Seeger, Ruth Crawford. *American Folk Songs for Children in Home, School, and Nursery School: A Book for Children, Parents, and Teachers*. New York: Doubleday, Zephyr, 1980.

Sendak, Maurice. *Where the Wild Things Are: 25th Anniversary Edition*. New York: HarperCollins, 1988.

Slobodkina, Esphyr. *Caps for Sale: A Tale of a Peddler, Some Monkeys, and Their Monkey Business*. New York: HarperCollins, 1947.

Spier, Peter. *The Star-Spangled Banner*. New York: Doubleday, 1973.

Van Allsburg, Chris. *The Polar Express*. Boston: Houghton Mifflin, 1985.

Voigt, Erna. *Peter and the Wolf*. (Adapted from the musical tale by Sergei Prokofiev.) Boston: David R. Godine, 1987.

Weil, Lisl. *Wolferl: The First Six Years in the Life of Wolfgang Amadeus Mozart, 1756–1762*. New York: Holiday House, 1991.

Westcott, Nadine Bernard. *I Know an Old Lady Who Swallowed a Fly*. Boston: Little, Brown; Joy Street Books, 1980.

———. *Skip to My Lou*. Boston: Little, Brown; Joy Street Books, 1989.

White, E. B. *Charlotte's Web*. New York: HarperCollins, 1952.

White, Elwyn B. *The Trumpet of the Swan*. New York: HarperCollins, 1970.

Wilder, Alec. *Lullabies and Night Songs*. New York: HarperCollins, 1965.

Williams, Margery. *The Velveteen Rabbit*. New York: Knopf, 1985.

Williams, Vera B. *Music, Music for Everyone*. New York: Greenwillow Books, 1984.

Winter, Jeanette. *Follow the Drinking Gourd*. New York: Knopf, 1988.

Wiseman, Ann. *Making Musical Things: Improvised Instruments*. New York: Macmillan, Scribner Books, 1979.

Wolfson, Evelyn. *From Abenaki to Zuni: A Dictionary of Native American Tribes*. New York: Walker, 1988.

Zemach, Harve. *Mommy, Buy Me a China Doll*. New York: Farrar, Straus and Giroux, Michael di Capua Books, 1975.

RECORDINGS FOR CHILDREN

Andrade, Sergio. *Sing Children Sing: Songs of Mexico*. Caedmon, 1980.

Bailey, Charity. *Follow the Sunset: A Beginning Geography Record with Nine Songs from Around the World*. Folkways, 1959.

Beall, Pamela Conn, and Susan Hagen Nipp. *Wee Sing Sing-Alongs*. Price/Stern/Sloan, 1990.

DeCormier, Robert. *Sing Children Sing: Songs of the United States of America*. Caedmon, 1977.

Horne, Marilyn, and Richard Robinson. *Lullabies from 'Round the World*. Rhythms Productions, 1956.

Jenkins, Ella. *Play Your Instruments and Make a Pretty Sound*. Folkways. 1968.

———. *Rhythms of Childhood*. Folkways, 1963.

———. *You'll Sing a Song and I'll Sing a Song*. Folkways, 1966.

Raffi. *Baby Beluga*. Shoreline, 1980.

———. *Corner Grocery Store and Other Singable Songs*. Shoreline, 1979.

———. *Rise and Shine*. Shoreline, 1982.

———. *Singable Songs for the Very Young*. Shoreline, 1976.

Seeger, Pete. *American Folk Songs for Children*. Folkways, 1954.

Siegmeister, Elie. *Invitation to Music*. Folkways, 1961.

Swift Eagle. *Pueblo Indians in Story, Song, and Dance*. Caedmon, 1972.

World Music Service. *Sound Effects*. Gateway, 1979 (cassettes), 1992 (CDs).

Subject Index